LEED

# LEED
# Materials
# A Resource Guide to Green Building

**Ari Meisel**

PRINCETON ARCHITECTURAL PRESS | NEW YORK

FSC
Mixed Sources
Product group from well-managed
forests and other controlled sources
Cert no. SGS-COC-003967
www.fsc.org
© 1996 Forest Stewardship Council

PUBLISHED BY:
Princeton Architectural Press
37 East 7th Street
New York, NY 10003

For a free catalog of books, call 1-800-722-6657
Visit our website at www.papress.com

All images courtesy of the respective product
manufacturer.

EDITOR: Linda Lee
DESIGNER: Paul Wagner

DISCLAIMER:
*Princeton Architectural Press and the author make
no warranties and representations concerning
these products or their use. The products included
in this book are not endorsed by the U.S. Green
Building Council. LEED is a registered trademark
of the USGBC.*

SPECIAL THANKS TO:
Nettie Aljian, Bree Anne Apperley,
Sara Bader, Nicola Bednarek,
Janet Behning, Becca Casbon, Carina Cha,
Penny (Yuen Pik) Chu, Carolyn Deuschle,
Russell Fernandez, Pete Fitzpatrick,
Wendy Fuller, Jan Haux, Clare Jacobson,
Erin Kim, Aileen Kwun, Nancy Eklund Later,
Laurie Manfra, John Myers, Katharine Myers,
Dan Simon, Andrew Stepanian, Katie Stokien,
Jennifer Thompson, Joseph Weston, and
Deb Wood of Princeton Architectural Press
—Kevin C. Lippert, publisher

LIBRARY OF CONGRESS
CATALOGING-IN-PUBLICATION DATA
Meisel, Ari, 1982–
LEED materials : a resource guide to green
building / Ari Meisel.
    p.    cm.
Includes index.
ISBN 978-1-56898-885-6 (alk. paper)
1. Building materials—United States—
Directories. 2. Green products—United States—
Directories. 3. Leadership in Energy and
Environmental Design Green Building Rating
System. 4. Sustainable construction.  I. Title.
TH12.5.M45 2010
693.8—dc22
                                              2009025280

# Contents

# Foreword

Green is the new black and has been for nearly a decade. Although the roots of the green building movement trace back to the AIA's Committee on the Environment in the 1980s and the U.S. Green Building Council's (USGBC) rise to prominence in the 1990s, it has achieved mainstream recognition only in the early part of this millennium.

Green certifications for residential construction have been in existence for about twenty years, starting in Austin, Texas, and spreading to a number of states, and through various sustainability initiatives, including the National Association of Home Builders (NAHB), USGBC, Green Globes, and about a dozen others across the globe, from the German Sustainable Building Council (DGNB) to BRE Environmental Assessment Method (BREEAM) in the United Kingdom. The USGBC launched the first nationwide residential green building standard, Leadership in Energy and Environmental Design (LEED) for Homes (L/H), a year ago, following five years of development and a two-year pilot program—this is the initiative I have led as chair of the USGBC's LEED for Homes committee since 2003.

The L/H standard can be applied not only to houses, but also to townhouses, garden apartments, and multifamily and mixed-use housing up to six stories in height. Ari Meisel and I worked together and refined L/H applications to New York City housing, which has been at the forefront of LEED applications, with the largest number of projects being reviewed for LEED certification, thanks largely to support from the New York State Energy Research and Development Authority (NYSERDA).

As a relatively young man, Ari has taken on the task of building more efficient structures with gusto. The first green building project he worked on was awarded the LEED Gold certification. Since then he has embarked on residential, recreational, edu-cational, and municipal-scale projects. His LEED Pro blog has become an informative resource for people looking to choose appropriate materials for their projects. His materials-based approach to green building is intuitive and dynamic, providing concrete solutions to green problems.

This book will be a valuable resource for green building professionals and consumers.

Steven Winter, FAIA
Former Chairman,
U.S. Green Building Council

# Preface

When I was in college, I worked with a group of fellow students to create an entrepreneurship program, which helped give students the skills needed to start a business based on their own ideas. When we first began there was a constant debate about whether you can actually teach entrepreneurship, or if it was innate. The main argument for teaching entrepreneurship was not that someone could learn how to be a risk taker or come up with ideas they didn't have before. The goal was to give them the tools they needed to foster an idea, make it a reality, and, most importantly, make it a success.

My background is in technology and construction, two passions I have had ever since I was a little boy, dismantling computers and trying to build full-sized structures out of LEGOs. I started my next company, ARISE Development, one week after my twenty-first birthday. Its first project was the rehabilitation of a group of buildings from the 1880s into luxury lofts and retail spaces. History has always fascinated me, and the chance to preserve these historic buildings was a dream come true. I did not know it then, but this project would become the foundation for my work in green building.

I chose to pursue my work within the LEED framework because it was better organized than any other system I had seen, and its emphasis on directly improving the lives of everyone who comes into contact with the built environment is unmatched. In 2005 I began working on a mixed-use, office, and affordable housing development called the Water Mill Ateliers, which would become the second LEED Gold-rated building in Long Island. Each day of the project, I would come across a dozen innovative products that I thought could be incorporated, and I had no good way of keeping track of them all. I decided to start a blog, which I called LEED Pro (www.leedpro.com), and organized each item by the credit that it helped fulfill. This was just for my own use, but I quickly found that the site was getting a lot of visits, reaching over a thousand per day in less than six months. I also joined the LEED Committee of the U.S. Green Building Council's New York chapter as well as the L/H committee in New York. People started contacting me for advice on how to use these products, and I began consulting on green building and sustainable design under my newest company, LEED Pro. All the while, I realized that a lot of people wanted to go green but were intimidated by the process and not sure what materials they could use to meet the standards set out for them.

I didn't expect to become a green building specialist or to create a source of information on LEED that people would actually use, and certainly not to write a book on the subject. It wouldn't have happened if not for my wife, Anna. In the winter of 2007, my then fiancée and I were discussing my LEED Pro blog and its potential to be something bigger. In a moment of uncharacteristic shortsightedness, I considered the possibility of doing a paid subscription newsletter or something of that sort. She wouldn't hear of it and insisted that I collect the information and make a real book, or nothing at all.

This all-or-nothing way of pursuing everything I do was instilled in me at an early age. When my parents were looking to enroll me in primary school, they applied to only a single school. When I applied to college, I decided on the one school that I wanted to attend, and I wrote in my application as much. I decided that if I didn't get in, I was going to join the Navy. I contacted Princeton Architectural Press with the same zeal—it was all or nothing for me. I'm very happy that they saw potential in this project and gave it the green light.

I must thank my parents, Louis and Susan, and my mother-in-law, Elisabeth, who always have different perspectives, and without them I would never be able to understand my own.

I also want to thank Yvon Pasquarello, who provided excellent help with research and gathering images for this book. Finally, I'd like to give mention to the vast materials wonderland that is Material ConneXion, a global online library of materials, where instead of stacks of books they have the most innovative and jaw-dropping collection of materials you've never heard of.

# Introduction

Green building is not an exact science, and a lot of times there isn't a particular right or wrong answer. You need to be adaptable and find solutions for challenging and unexpected problems. To achieve this, it is important to understand the available tools and materials that can be incorporated into your project.

The USGBC is a nonprofit organization committed to a more sustainable way of building. It expands the use of green building techniques through education and support, and through its LEED Green Building Rating System. LEED ratings, which can be applied to all types of building projects, break down into five major categories: sustainable site development, water savings, energy efficiency, materials and resources selection, and indoor environmental quality.

The LEED rating system essentially works on a credit system. You meet certain criteria developed by the USGBC in water-use reduction, materials reuse, energy optimization, indoor air quality, and site selection and get a certain number of points for each LEED credit. There are four levels of certification: Certified, Silver, Gold, and Platinum. Individuals proficient in the rating systems for different types of buildings can get certified as LEED Accredited Professionals. LEED is certainly not the only green building system out there; it competes with Energy Star, Green Globes, the NAHB National Green Building Guidelines, and a handful of others. All of these systems focus on using recycled materials, filtering air, reducing the waste of resources, and other relevant green-building issues. What LEED does in a more comprehensive manner than other systems is focus on making a healthier, more pleasant environment for the inhabitants of those spaces, not just on helping Mother Earth.

LEED was developed in 1994 and has been growing steadily ever since, having gone through several revisions and acquiring more rating systems—like New Construction, Existing Buildings, Core and Shell, and Commercial Interiors—to apply to different kinds of projects.

Materials and products, when implemented properly in a project, are what make it possible to achieve most LEED credits. But as the USGBC does not certify products, the ideas and suggestions in this book are based on the experience I have gained working on a number of very different green building projects. The products included here do not cover every single LEED credit since certain ones only require purchasing standard hardware at a store. This book is about materials, interesting and innovative—and probably unfamiliar—materials. I've divided the book up by the CSI MasterFormat Division™ in order to use something familiar to people in the building industry and make finding the product easier. LEED rating systems are updated every two years; LEED Version 3 is the framework that these material selections are based on.

Every day we see in the news that the environment is in bad shape. People today focus their attention on the daily heat indexes and greenhouse-gas levels around them the way that past generations watched daily values of commodities or the growth of the national deficit. According to the scientific community, we've never experienced temperatures this hot or fluctuational. Air quality is at an all-time low, we are breathing toxins almost every second of every day, and there are more cases of respiratory illness than ever before. Workers are tired and less productive because they don't breathe fresh air or benefit from the nourishing rays of the sun.

Most experts say it's our fault that the environment has come to this. Regardless of fault, there is something we can do about it, starting with some small steps—from repainting a guest room with nontoxic paint to specifying concrete with recycled fly ash for a skyscraper. The environment encompasses the entire globe, and it's therefore difficult to associate with your daily life, but your minienvironment includes the bedroom, the bathroom, the car, and the office. These are the places we need to affect first and foremost if we are to have any hope of achieving a healthier global ecosystem.

Green has become a full-fledged industry in its own right. Once a passion of a few small groups who sought a cleaner, less-commercial way of life—whether in a cabin in Vermont or a tent in the Grand Canyon—*green* has

become a global buzzword. Eco-luxury has taken hold—you can enjoy all of the high-end products and materials you are used to and still be green. We've come a long way from when being green meant living in an earth-covered hut in the middle of the forest, using open fire for light and heat; now we can buy power from renewable sources such as wind farms and ocean turbines.

One of the main criticisms of the LEED rating system is that it is not regionalized, meaning that water savings equals something very different in Arizona than in Washington. It requires much more effort, and likely expense, to save the same amount of water in a dry climate than it does in a temperate one, yet the points awarded are the same. The newest version of the rating system takes this into consideration. LEED is a constantly evolving set of criteria and has gained such a critical mass that it will be the standard to follow for many years to come.

The purpose of this book is to help anyone build green. There are plenty of books that present innovative and unique materials or products, but knowing how and when to apply them is the hard part. When building a green project, if you apply a material in the wrong situation, you may not get credit for it. On the other hand, with a little insider knowledge, you can also use one material to get credit in two, three, or even more areas.

A product that reduces water usage is just as useful to someone attempting LEED certification as it is to the homeowner who wants a lower water bill. The products that are included are those with a very low learning curve—no new skills are required to use them, and they can be installed with little or no training. I also hope you will learn how a certain product can be a tool to help you achieve a credit even if it's not listed on the submittal documents. For example, foam sealant is not an item that would necessarily be indicated anywhere, but it will help seal air gaps and improve energy efficiency. Anyone can employ these materials and methods and take a real interest in improving the immediate environment in which he or she lives. Additionally, most of the products are readily available in most markets—but if you can't source a particular material mentioned here, I hope that the information presented will help you find a suitable substitute.

There are some terms and acronyms that come up a lot when dealing with building green. For instance, wood that has been certified by the Forest Stewardship Council, or FSC, has been harvested in a sustainably managed forest. VOCs, or volatile organic compounds, are the toxic things we find in many paints, adhesives, and sealants that can give people headaches and respiratory problems. R-value refers to the heat conductivity of a material or its ability to stop heat transfer—from the outside of a house, through the wall, to the inside, for example. Recycled content is divided into postconsumer and preconsumer categories, with preconsumer content counting for twice as much since it has gone through one more stage of its potential lifecycle. Generally speaking, something made from recycled material should be able to be recycled over and over again with ease. The solar reflectance index (SRI) of a material can create a heat-island effect, which results from surfaces soaking up heat during the day and releasing it at night, and wreaks havoc on the ecosystem. All of these terms will become more familiar to you as relate them to materials in this book.

*LEED Materials* does not focus on the philosophy of building green or the reasons why it's a good thing. Most people understand why going green is right, but in the end, it's the decisions that we make, the products and materials we choose, that will make a difference. It is not the politics or the philosophies but the physical materials that we live and work with everyday. That's what this book is about: choices. This book is the first step toward a healthier, more environmentally sensitive way of building.

# LEED Rating System

| | |
|---|---|
| **Sustainable Sites** | ◉ |
| **Water Efficiency** | ⬥ |
| **Energy & Atmosphere** | ✸ |
| **Materials & Resources** | ✚ |
| **Indoor Environmental Quality** | ⊞ |
| **Innovation in Design Process** | ✴ |
| **Regional Priority** | ✕ |

*Note: The LEED rating systems, including LEED for New Construction and Major Renovations reproduced on the following pages, is available for public use at the U.S. Green Building Council website. For additional information, go to usgbc.gov. The icons presented above and throughout the book, which are included as a quick reference guide, are not used by USGBC.*

## Sustainable Sites

⊙ **SS Prerequisite 1**
**Construction Activity Pollution Prevention**
INTENT: To reduce pollution from construction by controlling soil erosion, water sedimentation, and airborne dust generation.

⊙ **SS Credit 1**
**Site Selection**
INTENT: To avoid the development of inappropriate sites and reduce the environmental impact from the location of a building on a site. **1 point**

⊙ **SS Credit 2**
**Development Density and Community Connectivity**
INTENT: To channel development to urban areas with existing infrastructure, protect greenfields, and preserve habitat and natural resources. **5 points**

⊙ **SS Credit 3**
**Brownfield Redevelopment**
INTENT: To rehabilitate damaged sites where development is complicated by environmental contamination and to reduce pressure on undeveloped land. **1 point**

⊙ **SS Credit 4.1**
**Alternative Transportation–Public Tranportation Access**
INTENT: To reduce pollution and land development impacts from automobile use.
**6 points**

⊙ **SS Credit 4.2**
**Alternative Transportation–Bicycle Storage and Changing Rooms**
INTENT: To reduce pollution and land development impacts from automobile use.
**1 point**

⊙ **SS Credit 4.3**
**Alternative Transportation–Low-Emitting and Fuel-Efficient Vehicles**
INTENT: To reduce pollution and land development impacts from automobile use.
**3 points**

⊙ **SS Credit 4.4**
**Alternative Transportation–Parking Capacity**
INTENT: To reduce pollution and land development impacts from automobile use.
**2 points**

⊙ **SS Credit 5.1**

**Site Development–Protect or**
**Restore Habitat**
INTENT: To conserve existing natural areas
and restore damaged areas to provide habitat
and promote biodiversity. **1 point**

⊙ **SS Credit 5.2**

**Site Development–Maximize Open Space**
INTENT: To promote biodiversity by
providing a high ratio of open space to
development footprint. **1 point**

⊙ **SS Credit 6.1**

**Stormwater Design–Quantity Control**
INTENT: To limit disruption of natural
hydrology by reducing impervious cover,
increasing on-site infiltration, reducing or
eliminating pollution from stormwater runoff
and eliminating contaminants. **1 point**

⊙ **SS Credit 6.2**

**Stormwater Design–Quality Control**
INTENT: To limit disruption and pollution of
natural water flows by managing stormwater
runoff. **1 point**

⊙ **SS Credit 7.1**

**Heat Island Effect–Nonroof**
INTENT: To reduce heat islands to minimize
impacts on microclimates and human and
wildlife habitats. **1 point**

⊙ **SS Credit 7.2**

**Heat Island Effect–Roof**
INTENT: To reduce heat islands to minimize
impacts on microclimates and human and
wildlife habitats. **1 point**

⊙ **SS Credit 8**

**Light Pollution Reduction**
INTENT: To minimize light trespass from
the building and site, reduce sky-glow to
increase night sky access, improve nighttime
visibility through glare reduction and reduce
development impact from lighting
on nocturnal environments. **1 point**

# Water Efficiency

### ◆ WE Prerequisite 1
**Water Use Reduction**
INTENT: To increase water efficiency within buildings to reduce the burden on municipal water supply and wastewater systems.

### ◆ WE Credit 1
**Water Efficient Landscaping**
INTENT: To limit or eliminate the use of potable water or other natural surface or subsurface water resources available on or near the project site for landscape irrigation.
**2–4 points**

### ◆ WE Credit 2
**Innovative Wastewater Technologies**
INTENT: To reduce wastewater generation and potable water demand while increasing the local aquifer recharge. **2 points**

### ◆ WE Credit 3
**Water Use Reduction**
INTENT: To further increase water efficiency within buildings to reduce the burden on municipal water supply and wastewater systems. **2–4 points**

# Energy & Atmosphere

### ✳ EA Prerequisite 1
**Fundamental Commissioning of Building Energy Systems**
INTENT: To verify that the project's energy-related systems are installed, and calibrated to perform according to the owner's project requirements, basis of design and construction documents.

Benefits of commissioning include reduced energy use, lower operating costs, fewer contractor callbacks, better building documentation, improved occupant productivity and verification that the systems perform in accordance with the owner's project requirements.

### ✳ EA Prerequisite 2
**Minimum Energy Performance**
INTENT: To establish the minimum level of energy efficiency for the proposed building and systems to reduce environmental and economic impacts associated with excessive energy use.

### ✳ EA Prerequisite 3
**Fundamental Refrigerant Management**
INTENT: To reduce stratospheric ozone depletion.

* **EA Credit 1**
Optimize Energy Performance
INTENT: To achieve increasing levels of
energy performance beyond the prerequisite
standard to reduce environmental and
economic impacts associated with excessive
energy use. **1–19 points**

* **EA Credit 2**
On-site Renewable Energy
INTENT: To encourage and recognize
increasing levels of on-site renewable energy
self-supply to reduce environmental and
economic impacts associated with fossil fuel
energy use. **1–7 points**

* **EA Credit 3**
Enhanced Commissioning
INTENT: To begin the commissioning
process early in the design process and
execute additional activities after systems
performance verification is completed.
**2 points**

* **EA Credit 4**
Enhanced Refrigerant Management
INTENT: To reduce ozone depletion
and support early compliance with the
Montreal Protocol while minimizing direct
contributions to climate change. **2 points**

* **EA Credit 5**
Measurement and Verification
INTENT: To provide for the ongoing
accountability of building energy
consumption over time. **3 points**

* **EA Credit 6**
Green Power
INTENT: To encourage the development
and use of grid-source, renewable energy
technologies on a net zero pollution basis.
**2 points**

## Materials and Resources

+ **MR Prerequisite 1**

**Storage and Collection of Recyclables**

INTENT: To facilitate the reduction of waste generated by building occupants that is hauled to and disposed of in landfills.

+ **MR Credit 1.1**

**Building Reuse–Maintain Existing Walls, Floors and Roof**

INTENT: To extend the lifecycle of existing building stock, conserve resources, retain cultural resources, reduce waste and reduce environmental impacts of new buildings as they relate to materials manufacturing and transport. **1–3 points**

+ **MR Credit 1.2**

**Building Reuse–Maintain Interior Nonstructural Elements**

INTENT: To extend the lifecycle of existing building stock, conserve resources, retain cultural resources, reduce waste and reduce environmental impacts of new buildings as they relate to materials manufacturing and transport. **1 point**

+ **MR Credit 2**

**Construction Waste Management**

INTENT: To divert construction and demolition debris from disposal in landfills and incineration facilities. Redirect recyclable recovered resources back to the manufacturing process and reusable materials to appropriate sites. **1–2 points**

+ **MR Credit 3**

**Materials Reuse**

INTENT: To reuse building materials and products to reduce demand for virgin materials and reduce waste, thereby lessening impacts associated with the extraction and processing of virgin resources. **1–2 points**

+ **MR Credit 4**

**Recycled Content**

INTENT: To increase demand for building products that incorporate recycled content materials, thereby reducing impacts resulting from extraction and processing of virgin materials. **1–2 points**

## Indoor Environmental Quality

### + MR Credit 5
**Regional Materials**
INTENT: To increase demand for building materials and products that are extracted and manufactured within the region, thereby supporting the use of indigenous resources and reducing the environmental impacts resulting from transportation. **1–2 points**

### + MR Credit 6
**Rapidly Renewable Materials**
INTENT: To reduce the use and depletion of finite raw materials and long-cycle renewable materials by replacing them with rapidly renewable materials. **1 point**

### + MR Credit 7
**Certified Wood**
INTENT: To encourage environmentally responsible forest management. **1 point**

### ⊞ IEQ Prerequisite 1
**Minimum Indoor Air Quality Performance**
INTENT: To establish minimum indoor air quality (IAQ) performance to enhance indoor air quality in buildings, thus contributing to the comfort and well-being of the occupants. **1 point**

### ⊞ IEQ Prerequisite 2
**Environmental Tobacco Smoke (ETS) Control**
INTENT: To prevent or minimize exposure of building occupants, indoor surfaces and ventilation air distribution systems to environmental tobacco smoke (ETS). **1 point**

### ⊞ IEQ Credit 1
**Outdoor Air Delivery Monitoring**
INTENT: To provide capacity for ventilation system monitoring to help promote occupant comfort and well-being. **1 point**

### ⊞ IEQ Credit 2
**Increased Ventilation**
INTENT: To provide additional outdoor air ventilation to improve indoor air quality (IAQ) and promote occupant comfort, well-being and productivity. **1 point**

# Indoor Environmental Quality (continued)

### ⊞ IEQ Credit 3.1
**Construction Indoor Air Quality Management Plan–During Construction**
INTENT: To reduce indoor air quality (IAQ) problems resulting from construction or renovation and promote the comfort and well-being of construction workers and building occupants. **1 point**

### ⊞ IEQ Credit 3.2
**Construction Indoor Air Quality Management Plan–Before Occupancy**
INTENT: To reduce indoor air quality (IAQ) problems resulting from construction or renovation to promote the comfort and well-being of construction workers and building occupants. **1 point**

### ⊞ IEQ Credit 4.1
**Low-Emitting Materials–Adhesives and Sealants**
INTENT: To reduce the quantity of indoor air contaminants that are odorous, irritating and/or harmful to the comfort and well-being of installers and occupants. **1 point**

### ⊞ IEQ Credit 4.2
**Low-Emitting Materials–Paints and Coatings**
INTENT: To reduce the quantity of indoor air contaminants that are odorous, irritating and/or harmful to the comfort and well-being of installers and occupants. **1 point**

### ⊞ IEQ Credit 4.3
**Low-Emitting Materials–Flooring Systems**
INTENT: To reduce the quantity of indoor air contaminants that are odorous, irritating and/or harmful to the comfort and well-being of installers and occupants. **1 point**

### ⊞ IEQ Credit 4.4
**Low-Emitting Materials–Composite Wood and Agrifiber Products**
INTENT: To reduce the quantity of indoor air contaminants that are odorous, irritating and/or harmful to the comfort and well-being of installers and occupants. **1 point**

⊞ **IEQ Credit 5**

**Indoor Chemical and Pollutant Source Control**

INTENT: To minimize building occupant exposure to potentially hazardous particulates and chemical pollutants. **1 point**

⊞ **IEQ Credit 6.1**

**Controllability of Systems–Lighting**

INTENT: To provide a high level of lighting system control by individual occupants or groups in multi-occupant spaces (e.g., classrooms and conference areas) and promote their productivity, comfort and well-being. **1 point**

⊞ **IEQ Credit 6.2**

**Controllability of Systems–Thermal Comfort**

INTENT: To provide a high level of thermal comfort system control by individual occupants or groups in multi-occupant spaces (e.g., classrooms or conference areas) and promote their productivity, comfort and well-being. **1 point**

⊞ **IEQ Credit 7.1**

**Thermal Comfort–Design**

INTENT: To provide a comfortable thermal environment that promotes occupant productivity and well-being. **1 point**

⊞ **IEQ Credit 7.2**

**Thermal Comfort–Verification**

INTENT: To provide for the assessment of building occupant thermal comfort over time. **1 point**

⊞ **IEQ Credit 8.1**

**Daylight and Views–Daylight**

INTENT: To provide building occupants with a connection between indoor spaces and the outdoors through the introduction of daylight and views into the regularly occupied areas of the building. **1 point**

⊞ **IEQ Credit 8.2**

**Daylight and Views–Views**

INTENT: To provide building occupants a connection to the outdoors through the introduction of daylight and views into the regularly occupied areas of the building. **1 point**

## Innovation in Design

### ☀ ID Credit 1
**Innovation in Design**
INTENT: To provide design teams and projects the opportunity to achieve exceptional performance above the requirements set by the LEED Green Building Rating System and/or innovative performance in Green Building categories not specifically addressed by the LEED Green Building Rating System. **1–5 points**

### ☀ ID Credit 2
**LEED Accredited Professional**
INTENT: To support and encourage the design integration required by LEED to streamline the application and certification process. **1 point**

## Regional Priority

### ✕ RP Credit 1
**Regional Priority**
INTENT: To provide an incentive for the achievement of credits that address geographically-specific environmental priorities. **1–4 points**

# Point Scale for Certification

| | |
|---|---|
| **Certified** | **40–49 points** |
| **Silver** | **50–59 points** |
| **Gold** | **60–79 points** |
| **Platinum** | **80 points and above** |

100 base points (plus 6 possible Innovation in Design points and 4 Regional Priority points)

# 1

# SITE CONSTRUCTION

# ARXX ICF

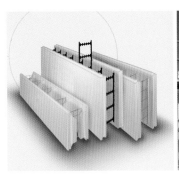

## LEED Credits

--------------------------------------

**✷ EA P2**
Minimum Energy Performance

**✷ EA 1**
Optimize Energy Performance

**✦ MR 2**
Construction Waste
Management

### Information
ARXX Corporation
800 Division Street
Cobourg, ON K9A 5V2
Canada
T 905 373 0004
F 905 373 8301
info@arxxbuild.com
www.arxxbuild.com

### What is it?
Insulated concrete forms

### Where can I use it?
Foundations, walls

### Why is it green?
ICF (insulated concrete form) systems make concrete walls
from what are essentially pieces of styrofoam held together
by plastic ties. The forms are stacked together in the desired
wall shape, after which the concrete mix (from any concrete
supplier) is poured in. The result is a concrete wall sandwiched
between two pieces of solid insulation. ARXX ICF uses a
customizable series of small, stackable components that can
be built up one piece at a time. In addition, any of the units
not used on site can be returned to the company, which
minimizes construction waste.

### Special Considerations
*These units utilize Styrofoam, which has no effect on LEED
credits, but may be unpleasant to hardcore environmentalists.*

# BioD-Mat 70

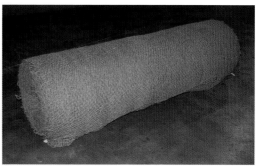

**What is it?**
Erosion-control blanket

**Where can I use it?**
Preventing soil erosion

**Why is it green?**
BioD-Mat 70 is a soil-retention product that forms a blanket made from coir, the fibrous material just inside the outer husk of a coconut. It is a strong, durable material. For a material to qualify as rapidly renewable, it must be harvested in a period shorter then 10 years from when it is planted; coir can be harvested every 7 weeks, all year round. The products have a useful life of 4-to-6 years, after which they will completely biodegrade into the underlying soil.

RoLanka, the company that manufactures BioD-Mat 70, sources its coir from Sri Lanka and weaves it into blankets. These blankets can be laid on soil areas during construction to protect against the destructive nature of demolition and heavy-duty vehicles. Since it will biodegrade over time, it can be left in place and will continue to provide soil-erosion protection until permanent vegetation can take hold or some other hardscape surface is put in place.

## LEED Credits

⊙ **SS P1**
Construction Activity
Pollution Protection

✦ **MR 2**
Construction Waste
Management

✦ **MR 6**
Rapidly Renewable Materials

**Information**
RoLanka International
T  770 506 8211
F  770 506 0391
rolanka@rolanka.com
www.rolanka.com

# Buffalograss

## LEED Credits

⊙ **SS 6.1**
Stormwater Design—
Quantity Control

💧 **WE 1**
Water Efficient Landscaping

### Information
Todd Valley Farms
P.O. Box 202
Mead, NE 68041
T  402 624 6385
info@toddvalleyfarms.com
www.toddvalleyfarms.com

**What is it?**
Low-maintenance lawn covering

**Where can I use it?**
Lawns, vegetated roofs

**Why is it green?**
Buffalograss is the only turfgrass native to the United States and is an incredibly resilient, low-maintenance species of lawn grass. Buffalograss will grow lush and full with just ¼ inch of rainfall per week. Depending on the geographic location of the project, this could eliminate the need for any artificial irrigation, because regular rainfall would be sufficient. And if the project is located in a dry area, the grass will only need minimal amounts of water to provide enough irrigation. Using grass instead of hardscape materials such as concrete and asphalt allows stormwater to drain into the ground instead of running off the site.

Todd Valley Farms offers four varieties of buffalograss, each for a different climate. As an added benefit, buffalograss grows very slowly, and the highest any of the varieties will grow is 6 inches, which means you can reduce or eliminate the need for mowing. The turf also has very low levels of pollen and is naturally resistant to insects.

# DirtGlue

### What is it?
Soil-stabilization polymer

### Where can I use it?
Preventing soil erosion, natural paths

### Why is it green?
DirtGlue is a compound that makes soil particles bind to form a flexible film over the soil. Construction activity can cause soil degradation and can pollute groundwater and nearby streams. DirtGlue takes the dust that trucks kick up that might enter the air during construction to create a film that prevents soil erosion. DirtGlue is water soluble and nonhazardous, so it can be applied anywhere, including near river beds, without harming land animals or aquatic life. The compound comes in two versions: DirtGlue Light is applied to the surface of the soil for basic protection from mechanical damage from vehicles or equipment, wind, or water erosion, and can be used to temporarily cap dirt piles. DirtGlue Industrial is mixed with the soil to form a sturdier surface that can withstand the punishing effects of heavy construction vehicles and long-term abuse.

### Special Considerations
*The compound may need to be reapplied after heavy usage.*

## LEED Credits

⊙ **SS P1**
Construction Activity
Pollution Protection

### Information
DirtGlue Enterprises
83 Middle Road
Amesbury, MA 01913
T 978 388 3312
F 508 861 0550
customerservice@dirtglue.com
www.dirtglue.com

# Drivable Grass

## LEED Credits

### ⊙ SS P1
Construction Activity
Pollution Prevention

### ⊙ SS 6.1
Stormwater Design—
Quantity Control

### ⊙ SS 7.1
Heat Island Effect—Nonroof

### Information
Soil Retention Products, Inc.
2501 State Street
Carlsbad, CA 92008
T  800 346 7995
sales@soilretention.com
www.soilretention.com

**What is it?**
Paving system

**Where can I use it?**
Parking areas, driveways

**Why is it green?**
Drivable Grass consists of flexible mats of small concrete blocks that can be laid down by anyone as it requires no special skills. They come in roughly 2 x 2 foot sections, which can be used to make anything from a small driveway to a large parking area. The system is completely modular—you just lay them down one next to the other, then grass freely grows between the blocks, filling in the spaces while maintaining an even, sturdy surface for vehicles to traverse. The mats can be installed during construction for soil retention, then be left in place as a permanent surface. The spaces between the concrete allow for unrestricted drainage of stormwater and also eliminate the heat-island effect that dark asphalt can produce.

**Special Considerations**
*Some municipalities will not allow this type of surface because it may violate specific building codes or hinder handicap access.*

# Durisol ICF

### What is it?
Cement-bonded wood-fiber-insulated concrete forms

### Where can I use it?
Load-bearing and non-load-bearing walls

### Why is it green?
From a distance Durisol ICFs look like any regular concrete building block. However, Durisol uses wood waste from factories—a preconsumer recycled product—which, in this case, is a good thing because this source guarantees a consistent supply of base material. The waste is put through a wood chipper and then mixed with Portland cement as a binder. This mixture is then molded into standard concrete-blocked shapes.

Typical polystyrene ICFs have the majority of their insulation in the interior of the form. Also, the inherent weakness of Styrofoam makes them susceptible to blowouts when they are filled with concrete. Durisol blocks have most of their insulation on the exterior, stopping heat transfer before it gets into the structure, which gives them superior thermal-insulating values. Their rigid, weight-supporting form means there is no risk of a blowout during setup.

Durisol ICFs are made of 80 percent recycled content and are completely recyclable. Additionally, they are impervious to mold growth or insect infestations. They are very easy to install since regular carpentry tools can be used. Finished drywall can be easily screwed into the blocks, and due to their porous and fibrous surface, stucco or plaster can adhere very well.

## LEED Credits

✴ **EA P2**
Minimum Energy Performance

✴ **EA 1**
Optimize Energy Performance

✦ **MR 2**
Construction Waste Management

✦ **MR 4**
Recycled Content

### Information
Durisol Building Systems, Inc.
505 York Boulevard
Suite 2
Hamilton, Ontario L8R 3K4
Canada
T 905 521 0999
F 905 521 8658
info@durisolbuild.com
www.durisolbuild.com

# Eco-Cement

## LEED Credits

⊙ **SS 7.1**
Heat Island Effect—Nonroof

✦ **MR 2**
Construction Waste
Management

✦ **MR 4**
Recycled Content

✴ **ID 1**
Innovation in Design

**Information**
TecEco Pty. Ltd.
497 Main Road
Glenorchy
Tasmania 7010
Australia
T +61 3 62497868
F +61 3 62730010
www.tececo.com

**What is it?**
$CO_2$-absorbing cement.

**Where can I use it?**
Anywhere you use cement

**Why is it green?**
Concrete manufacturing is one of the worst producers of greenhouses gases in the world. Each year, it generates more carbon pollution than the entire aviation industry—5 percent of all the world's emissions.

TecEco introduces magnesia into their concrete mix along with recycled materials like fly ash. When magnesia is mixed in with the Portland cement, it takes on an amazing property, and as it cools and cures, it absorbs $CO_2$ and sequesters it permanently. Each kilogram of Eco-Cement made results in net carbon emissions of 0.23 kilograms. Constructing a building with Eco-Cement blocks or paving a parking lot with the light-colored cement (which also eliminates the heat-island effect) helps remove greenhouse gases from the atmosphere. The credits that LEED gives for this material are not related to its most important property of helping to fight global warming.

# Enkadrain

**What is it?**
Soil-retention system

**Where can I use it?**
Soil retention, green roofing, drainage, sound dampening

**Why is it green?**
Enkadrain is a multilayered drainage composite that can be installed during construction to protect natural soil deposits and give them some structure so they do not run off and pollute neighboring properties, municipal water systems, or natural water sources. Stormwater also drains through the Enkadrain very effectively since the material creates a hydrostastic space between it and the dirt. The back of this material acts as a natural filter for this stormwater, retaining particulates of a certain size and preventing them from polluting groundwater. The Enkadrain can be left in place after construction, where it will act as a stable growing medium for anything planted on top. This trait makes it equally suited to mitigating the heat-island effect on vegetated roofs and on the ground.

## LEED Credits

⊙ **SS P1**
Construction Activity Pollution Prevention

⊙ **SS 6.1**
Stormwater Design—Quantity Control

⊙ **SS 6.2**
Stormwater Design—Quality Control

⊙ **SS 7.1**
Heat Island Effect—Nonroof

⊙ **SS 7.2**
Heat Island Effect—Roof

**Information**
Colbond, Inc.
Sand Hill Road
P.O. Box 1057
Enka, NC 28728
T 828 665 5050 / 800 365 7391
F 828 665 5009
enka-engineered@colbond.com
www.colbond-usa.com

# EnviroSCAPE

## LEED Credits

⊙ **SS 6.1**
Stormwater Design—
Quantity Control

⊙ **SS 6.2**
Stormwater Design—
Quality Control

✛ **MR 4**
Recycled Content

**Information**
EnviroGLAS
7704 San Jacinto Place
Suite 200
Plano, TX 75024
T 972 608 3790
communications@
enviroglasproducts.com
www.enviroglasproducts.com

**What is it?**
Mulch made from recycled materials

**Where can I use it?**
Plantings, parking areas, walkways

**Why is it green?**
EnviroGLAS takes bottles and porcelain out of the waste stream and crushes and polishes the recycled material to resemble gravel, but without any sharp edges. As mulch, this material does not absorb any water, but it holds water in place because it creates tight spaces that trap the water, reducing evaporation. (Water also "sticks" to glass a little.) As a result, plants get more of the irrigation they need without the additional use of fresh, possibly potable water. And since the material does not absorb water and is already heavier than other natural mulch, it will not wash away in storms. The gravel-like surface also acts as a natural filter for large particles that might otherwise pollute groundwater. Furthermore, because it is glass and completely inert, it will not harbor the growth of weeds or insect colonies.

# ForeverLawn

**What is it?**
Synthetic turf system with built-in drainage

**Where can I use it?**
Landscaping, rooftops, balconies, athletic fields

**Why is it green?**
BioBalance polymers, which make up the blades of grass, are made from soybean plants, a rapidly renewable resource. The backing also contains Celceram, a recovered (likely from carpet recycling) natural mineral, used to increase product stability against foot traffic. The secondary backing is a 100 percent postconsumer recycled, a permeable fabric made from plastic bottles and meant to work with soil for retention, drainage, or a barrier. This backing allows stormwater to drain through easily and acts as a natural filter for large particulate matter. Since ForeverLawn is not real living grass, it does not support insect populations, does not require fertilizers or pesticides, and will never need watering. Outdoor water use, such as watering large fields of grass, makes up a large part of total water consumption in the world—the application of ForeverLawn will significantly reduce this waste.

## LEED Credits

⊙ **SS 6.1**
Stormwater Design—
Quantity Control

⊙ **SS 6.2**
Stormwater Design—
Quality Control

◆ **WE 1**
Water Efficient Landscaping

✛ **MR 4**
Recycled Content

✛ **MR 6**
Rapidly Renewable Materials

**Information**
ForeverLawn, Inc.
4500 Bogan Avenue NE
Albuquerque, NM 87109
T 866 992 7876
F 866 212 1925
contact@foreverlawn.com
www.foreverlawn.com

# Fortrac 30G

## LEED Credits

⊙ **SS P1**
Construction Activity Pollution
Prevention

**Information**
HUESKER Inc.
P.O. Box 411529
Charlotte, NC 28241
T 704 588 5500 / 800 942 9418
F 704 588 5988
marketing@hueskerinc.com
www.huesker.com

**What is it?**
Woven-mesh reinforcement for grassy slopes

**Where can I use it?**
Vegetated slopes, preventing soil erosion

**Why is it green?**
When doing green construction, it is important to control soil erosion, waterway sedimentation, and airborne dust. Fortrac 30G is a soil-reinforcement mesh made from coated polyester yarn woven into an interlocking grid pattern. It comes in large rolls, and it is simply laid in place by hand over any areas of vegetation and loose dirt. The mesh will effectively lock those areas down and prevent erosion by holding the soil together. This material is not susceptible to insects, UV radiation, extreme weather, or chemical products.

# Gavin Historical Bricks

**What is it?**
Reclaimed bricks and pavers

**Where can I use it?**
Driveways, patios

**Why is it green?**
Historically, large, empty merchant ships coming to America from Europe would use cobblestones, also known as Belgian blocks, as ballast. Upon arrival, they would dump the blocks and load up with cargo for the return trip. The thousands of durable, abandoned granite blocks made excellent street-paving material, and that's just what most of the cities on the East Coast used them for in the past.

Gavin Historical Bricks reclaims these pavers after the completion of street work—during which the cobblestones are ripped up and asphalt put down—as well as bricks from streets and buildings all over the country. The company cleans them up and sells these wonderful specimens. Visually, the nicest feature of this material is its irregularity, which is uncommon today due to modern kilns or carving methods. When pavers are used for a driveway or other hardscape area, the space between each paver allows stormwater to drain through, avoiding runoff.

**Special Considerations**
*If the pavers are a light color, they will probably help you qualify for a heat-island-effect credit since they will reflect heat rather then holding it during the day and releasing it at night.*

## LEED Credits

⊙ **SS 6.1**
Stormwater Design—
Quantity Control

⊙ **SS 7.1**
Heat Island Effect—Nonroof

✛ **MR 3**
Materials Reuse

**Information**
Gavin Historical Bricks
2050 Glendale Road
Iowa City, IA 52245
T 319 354 5251
F 319 688 3086
info@historicalbricks.com
www.historicalbricks.com

# GraniteCrete

## LEED Credits

⊙ **SS 6.1**
Stormwater Design—
Quantity Control

⊙ **SS 6.2**
Stormwater Design—
Quality Control

⊙ **SS 7.1**
Heat Island Effect—Nonroof

✛ **MR 4**
Recycled Content

### Information
GraniteCrete
4 Buena Vista Del Rio
Carmel Valley, CA 93924
T 800 670 0849
info@granitecrete.com
www.granitecrete.com

**What is it?**
Pavement alternative

**Where can I use it?**
Walkways, paths, driveways

**Why is it green?**
GraniteCrete is a sustainable hardscape solution with multiple benefits. It is made from a mixture of colorants, natural clays, and preconsumer recycled granite—the exact specifications of which are a trade secret. The material costs roughly one-third of what concrete does and is installed by simply laying it over a bed of gravel and then compacting it, making it immediately available for use. No special tools or skills are needed to install it, and it can be removed with a pickaxe if the need should arise. The mixture is available in six different earth tones that negate the heat-island effect, and its sandlike composition allows stormwater to drain through rather then running off and polluting other areas. Because of its porous nature, it acts as an effective filter for waste that would otherwise pollute the aquifer.

# Gravelpave²

**What is it?**
Soil retention and alternative paving system.

**Where can I use it?**
Parking lots, driveways, walkways

**Why is it green?**
Gravelpave² is a structure onto which loose gravel is placed to create a solid surface that allows stormwater to drain while filtering larger pollutants before they can infiltrate groundwater. Also, using a light-colored stone, such as a light gray crushed peastone, can prevent the heat-island effect that is created by more traditional paving surfaces, such as black asphalt. Using gravel is also much more cost effective than asphalt or concrete, contrary to the common conception that building green has to be expensive.

**Special Considerations**
*Some municipalities will not allow this type of surface because it may violate specific building codes or hinder handicap access.*

## LEED Credits

⊙ **SS 6**
Stormwater Design—
 Quantity Control

⊙ **SS 6.2**
Stormwater Design—
 Quality Control

⊙ **SS 7.1**
Heat Island Effect—Nonroof

**Information**
Invisible Structures
1600 Jackson Street
Suite 310
Golden, CO 80401
T 303 233 8383
dustin@invisiblestructures.com
www.invisiblestructures.com

# GreenLoxx

## LEED Credits

⊙ **SS P1**
Construction Activity
Pollution Prevention

### Information
Filtrexx
35481 Grafton Eastern Road
Grafton, OH 44044
T  440 926 2607
info@filtrexx.com
www.filtrexx.com

### What is it?
Soil-retention system

### Where can I use it?
Construction site protection, permanent soil retention

### Why is it green?
Integrating the company's trademarked FilterSoxx netting and the Growing Media fascia, the GreenLoxx system can be used to create a retaining wall for temporary or permanent site protection and beautification. The system allows you to create a vertical or near-vertical agriculture wall that can help stop soil erosion, stormwater runoff, and stream pollution. The materials are completely customizable, so they will work for any site or any size, and with any type of vegetation.

# Insulspan SIP

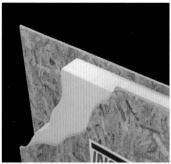

**What is it?**

Structural insulated panel system

**Where can I use it?**

Walls, floors, roofs

**Why is it green?**

SIPs (structural insulated panels) are a major step forward in integrated building systems. They put the builder halfway between starting from scratch and having to bring in a pre-fabricated structure completed offsite. Once architectural drawings are submitted, these panels, consisting of two oriented strand boards (OSBs) laminated to an expanded polystyrene (EPS) core, are manufactured at Insulspan's factory and delivered to the job site. The panels are precut at the factory with windows and doors and fit together like a big jigsaw puzzle. There is very little to learn in the way of putting these in place, and standard tools can be used to nail or screw the panels together, producing a building exterior with no air leakage, a higher than average effective R-value, and minimal waste. Structural insulated panels are building blocks for contractors.

**Special Considerations**

*These panels are predesigned and produced offsite, making changes a little difficult.*

## LEED Credits

✱ **EA P2**

Minimum Energy Performance

✛ **MR 2**

Construction Waste Management

**Information**

Insulspan
P.O. Box 38
Blissfield, MI 49228
T  517 486 4844
F  517 486 2056
insulspan@insulspan.com
www.insulspan.com

# Integrity Block

## LEEDCredits

⁕ **EA P2**
Minimum Energy Performance

⁕ **EA 1**
Optimize Energy Performance

✛ **MR 4**
Recycled Content

✛ **MR 5**
Regional Materials

### Information
Integrity Block
4966 El Camino Real
Suite 223
Los Altos, CA 94022
T  650 641 3104
F  650 963 1544
info@integrityblock.com
www.integrityblock.com

**What is it?**
Recycled content masonry unit

**Where can I use it?**
Outside entryways

**Why is it green?**
The Integrity Block technology is based on thousands of years of building with earth, such as the adobe and rammed-earth techniques. Integrity Blocks are made of a proprietary soil blend from by-products of quarry mining with up to 50 percent preconsumer recycled content. They come in the same forms as standard concrete masonry blocks, so there is no learning curve to install them, and they fulfill a variety of construction needs. The blocks are made from materials sourced near the company's facility, and Integrity Block is working on opening facilities around the United States so that all projects will be able to earn Regional Materials credit for using Integrity Blocks. According to tests performed by the company, the blocks improved thermal transfer resistance, when compared to standard wood member framing, and can help optimize energy performance as well.

# J-DRain GRS

**What is it?**
Drainage base for vegetated surfaces

**Where can I use it?**
Roofs, hardscapes

**Why is it green?**
The J-DRain GRS is a preassembled, ready-to-install drainage base for vegetated roofs and hardscapes. It is made from preconsumer polystyrene recycled content and can help you achieve almost ten LEED credits. In order to achieve credits relating to restoring a habitat and for maximizing open space, you need to restore or create vegetated space equal to the building footprint or a percent of it, depending on local zoning. Drainage cups with preattached filter fabric are laid down on a roof or another surface, after which a planting medium can be applied, and vegetation will begin to grow.

The vegetated roof will soak up and use the majority of any rainwater that falls on it, and excess water will be stored in the drainage cups of the J-DRain until it is needed. These units can hold 1.1 gallons for every 10 square feet; beyond that capacity the water will be filtered by the filter fabric and run freely under these drainage cores.

A green roof mitigates the heat-island effect. Studies show that it can reduce cooling needs by upward of 30 percent simply by blocking thermal energy from the sun. That energy isn't simply reflected back and lost; the vegetation uses it to grow stronger and thicker, which increases the effectiveness of the system.

**Special Considerations**
*Make sure your roof can support the weight of the vegetated roof system, planting medium, and water.*

## LEED Credits

⊙ **SS 5.1** Site Development—Protect or Restore Habitat

⊙ **SS 5.2** Site Development—Maximize Open Space

⊙ **SS 6.1** Stormwater Design—Quantity Control

⊙ **SS 6.2** Stormwater Design—Quality Control

⊙ **SS 7.1**
Heat Island Effect—Nonroof

⊙ **SS 7.2**
Heat Island Effect—Roof

✳ **EA P2** Minimum Energy Performance

✳ **EA 1**
Optimize Energy Performance

✛ **MR 4**
Recycled Content

**Information**
JDR Enterprises, Inc.
292 South Main Street, Suite 200
Alpharetta, GA 30004
T 770 442 1461
F 800 843 7569
info@j-drain.com
www.j-drain.com

# NewGrass

## LEED Credits

◉ **SS 6.1**
Stormwater Design—
Quantity Control

◉ **SS 6.2**
Stormwater Design—
Quality Control

◆ **WE 1**
Water Efficient Landscaping

✚ **MR 2**
Construction Waste
Management

✚ **MR 4**
Recycled Content

✚ **MR 6**
Rapidly Renewable Materials

### Information
NewGrass, LLC
515 Houston Street
Suite 806
Fort Worth, TX 76102
T 866 583 5602
info@newgrass.com
www.newgrass.com

**What is it?**
Artificial grass

**Where can I use it?**
Lawns, roofs, vegetated areas

**Why is it green?**
NewGrass looks and feels remarkably like real grass, and if you you didn't already know, you wouldn't really notice that it is artificial. The backing is made with compounds derived from soybeans, a rapidly renewable source, while the blades are made from postconsumer recycled polyethylene terephthalate from soda and water bottles. The entire setup is completely recyclable, and the company will pick it up and recycle it at the end of its lifespan. Since the grass is artificial, it does not require any irrigation, and the backing acts as an efficient filter and drainage system for stormwater.

The grass comes in four quality levels, Rye, Premium Rye, Fescue, and Sport, for different applications like general use, pets, and sports fields.

**Special Considerations**
*Though this material looks very much like its natural counterpart, some landscape architects may not accept it.*

# Permapave Filtration Grate

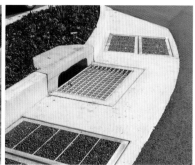

**What is it?**
Stormwater filtration grate

**Where can I use it?**
Storm drains

**Why is it green?**
Permapave makes permeable pavers from natural stone. They allow water to flow through at a rate of 30 liters per second per unit and work as an excellent pollutant filter. They can be laid down as standard pavers over a large area; the company also offers catch basin drains and curb units. The units filter 100 percent of large pollutants like leaves or trash, while the curbside unit can also prevent 60 percent of phosphorus, 70 percent of heavy metals, and 98 percent of hydrocarbons from entering the groundwater supply. Allowing stormwater to drain into the ground rather than running off into municipal lines is good start, and these efficient filtering properties of the pavers/grates also protect the aquifer.

## LEED Credits

⊙ **SS 6.1**
Stormwater Design—
Quantity Control

⊙ **SS 6.2**
Stormwater Design—
Quality Control

**Information**
Permapave USA Corp.
P.O. Box 665
Jericho, NY 11753
T 516 584 2110
info@permapave.com
www.permapave.com

# Rubberific Mulch and NuPlay

## LEED Credits

⊙ **SS P1**
Construction Activity
Pollution Prevention

⊙ **SS 6.1**
Stormwater Design—
Quantity Control

✛ **MR 4**
Recycled Content

### Information
International Mulch Company
One Mulch Lane
Bridgeton, MO 63044
T  314 336 1030
www.internationalmulch.com

**What is it?**
Mulch and playground surfacing made from recycled rubber

**Where can I use it?**
Mulch, planters, parking areas, edging, playgrounds

**Why is it green?**
The International Mulch Company makes several products using 100 percent recycled rubber tires. Recycled rubber mulch is better than wood mulch in several respects: It never has to be replaced (wood typically needs to be remulched twice per year). It is five times heavier then wood, so it will not float away or erode after heavy rains. It does not promote any type of insect or mold growth and allows stormwater to drain more efficiently because it is completely nonabsorbent.

Rubberific mulch can be made in any color, and the product line includes recycled rubber borders and tree rings, which can help prevent soil and plant life erosion. It can also be used as a base material for playgrounds, reducing injuries.

# VAST Pavers

**What is it?**
Recycled-content pavers

**Where can I use it?**
Parking lots, patios, driveways, walkways, roof decks

**Why is it green?**
VAST Pavers are made of 95 percent recycled content from scrap plastic and tires. They come in permeable and nonpermeable versions for different applications and offer a whole host of potential LEED credits. VAST Enterprises offers a closed-loop recycling program, in which the user returns the pavers to the company instead of sending them to a landfill when they are no longer needed. The company's manufacturing facility is located in Minneapolis, Minnesota, and all of the material is obtained locally. Projects located within five hundred miles may qualify for a regional materials credit.

If used to create a surface, such as a parking lot, the permeable pavers will allow stormwater to seep through and into the ground, avoiding run-off. Both versions of the paver are eligible for a number of credits, but the permeable one acts as a natural filter and can additionally achieve both Stormwater Design credits with one product.

Specific available colors that VAST offers, such as red wood and water wheel, can help meet the SRI threshold of 29 needed to prevent a heat-island effect.

## LEED Credits

⊙ **SS 6.1**
Stormwater Design—
Quantity Control

⊙ **SS 6.2**
Stormwater Design—
Quality Control

⊙ **SS 7.1**
Heat Island Effect—Nonroof

⊙ **SS 7.2**
Heat Island Effect—Roof

✦ **MR 4**
Recycled Content

✦ **MR 2**
Construction Waste
Management

✦ **MR 5**
Regional Materials

### Information
VAST Enterprises
1828 Marshall Street NE
Suite 15A
Minneapolis, MN 55418
T 612 234 8958
F 612 706 0017
sales@vastpavers.com
www.vastpavers.com

# XPotential Impact-Posts and Impact-Curbs

## LEED Credits

**+ MR 2**
Construction Waste
Management

**+ MR 4**
Recycled Content

### Information
XPotential Products, Inc.
(head office)
P.O. Box 126
St. Boniface Postal Station
Winnipeg, Manitoba R2H 3B4
Canada
T  800 863 6619
F  204 224 4678
sales@xpotentialproducts.com
www.xpotentialproducts.com

### What is it?
A composite material made of recycled content

### Where can I use it?
Parking designation, curbing, edging, retaining walls, fencing, walkways

### Why is it green?
Impact-Posts and Impact-Curbs are two products in the XPotential line of heavy lumber alternatives. They are made completely from postconsumer recycled plastic by-products generated from the thousands of automobiles that are sent to the dumps every year. These products can be cut, drilled, fastened, and painted like wood, but last decades longer. They are not susceptible to infestation or fading—and can be used like any other wood alternative. Due to their recycled composition, they are easily recyclable.

# Zipblocks

### What is it?
Interlocking building blocks

### Where can I use it?
Furniture, retaining walls, walkways, bridges, aqueducts, walls, roofs

### Why is it green?
Zipblocks are difficult to describe because they are so simple, yet infinitely versatile. They are interlocking building blocks of various materials and sizes, based on a simple cube lattice system—the same structure behind the form of crystals. They are like large-scale LEGO blocks. The product comes in two shapes, blocks and lugs, and these shapes fit together to make a perfectly aligned structural form that uses zero adhesives and can be deconstructed and used to form a completely different structure. They can be made of almost any kind of material, from recycled metal to scrap wood, and since they use a mechanical locking system, Zipblocks of different materials can be attached to each other: styrofoam to wood to steel, for example. Even a shipping container can be constructed out of these blocks so that its components can be disassembled on site and reused to build a structure. The product can be faced with tiles or brick or even solar panels.

### Special Considerations
*These blocks are not in mass production; lead time may be a consideration. Because this is a very new material, size and weight limitations are not available, although bridges have been built using the product.*

## LEED Credits

✦ **MR 1.1**
Building Reuse—Maintain Existing Walls, Floors and Roof

✦ **MR 1.2**
Building Reuse—Maintain Interior Nonstructural Elements

✦ **MR 2**
Construction Waste Management

✦ **MR 4**
Recycled Content

⊞ **IEQ 4.1**
Low-Emitting Materials: Adhesives and Sealants

✳ **ID 1**
Innovation in Design

### Information
Zipblocks LLC
Chamber of Commerce Building
330 South Tryon Street
Suite 400
Charlotte, NC 28202
T 704 383 3944
F 704 383 6545
info@zipblocks.com
www.zipblocks.com

# 2

# WOOD & PLASTICS

# Bamboo Snapping Deck Tiles

 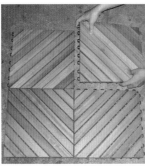 

## LEED Credits

⊙ **SS 6.1**
Stormwater Design—
Quantity Control

⊙ **SS 7.1**
Heat Island Effect—Nonroof

⊙ **SS 7.2**
Heat Island Effect—Roof

✦ **MR 6**
Rapidly Renewable Materials

✦ **MR 7**
Certified Wood

### Information

VIFAH U.S. Showroom
335 West 35th Street
Floor 7
New York, NY 10001
T  888 833 8674
F  866 213 5328
sales@vifah.com
www.vifah.com

**What is it?**
Bamboo deck tiles

**Where can I use it?**
Roof decking, ground decks

**Why is it green?**
Bamboo grows so rapidly that its progress is visible to the naked eye. It makes an ideal building material since it can be harvested very quickly. VIFAH sources its bamboo from FSC-certified forests, mainly in Asia, to produce these beautiful deck tiles.

The slats are placed on a plastic mesh that is raised slightly off the ground, which allows air to circulate and aids in the evaporation of standing water. This same feature makes it very easy for water to drain through, helping with stormwater control and capture, so it may be reused for landscaping or other domestic uses.

The tiles work as well on the ground as they do on roof decks. Since the prestained slats have a high SRI, they help mitigate any heat-island effect that might otherwise be caused by a darker, more solar-absorbing material. These tiles go in place and snap together without the use of any tools or special skills. They can be used both indoors and outside, and can be cut to follow the shape of a room or a border and still maintain their integrity and interlocking ability.

# Beach Pebble

**What is it?**
Cabinet hardware

**Where can I use it?**
Cabinets

**Why is it green?**
SpectraDécor makes a line of cabinet knobs called Beach Pebble. The knobs are mounted on lead-free pewter, and while they may look like beautifully smooth natural stones plucked from the beach, they are not at all. The knobs are made from 100 percent recycled glass. They are available in ten standard colors, but each of the company's pieces is made to order, and custom colors are available.

## LEED Credits

**✦ MR 4**
Recycled Content

**Information**
SpectraDécor
T 800 550 1986
info@spectradecor.com
www.spectradecor.com

# Bioline

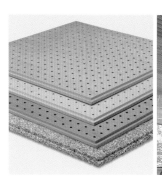

## LEED Credits

✦ **MR 4**
Recycled Content

⊞ **IEQ 4.4**
Low-Emitting Materials—
Composite Wood and
Agrifiber Products

### Information

Pinta Acoustic, Inc.
2601 49th Avenue North
Suite 400
Minneapolis, MN 55430
T 612 355 4250 / 800 662 0032
(United States and Canada only)
F 612 355 4255
sales@pinta-acoustic.com
www.pinta-acoustic.com

**What is it?**
Wood ceiling tiles

**Where can I use it?**
Ceilings

**Why is it green?**
Bioline ceiling tiles come in two lines, Solid Finish and Organic Texture. The Solid Finish line has finish veneers like maple, bamboo, and cherry, and contains 70 percent recycled content; while the Organic Texture line comes in three different shades of natural wood and contains 80 percent recycled content. Organic Texture can provide acoustic insulation by reducing reverberation by up to 80 percent. The recycled content is preconsumer, so it will only count for half in the credits, and the panels have no added urea formaldehyde. Urea formaldehyde has been shown to be highly toxic to our respiratory systems. The panels come in standard sizes of 2 x 2 feet, 2 x 4 feet, and 2 x 6 feet, or can be custom-made.

# DriTac 7500 Eco-Urethane

**What is it?**
Nontoxic flooring adhesive

**Where can I use it?**
Flooring

**Why is it green?**
DriTac 7500 is a wood-flooring adhesive that complies with the Low-Emitting Materials credit because it contains absolutely no VOCs and is also completely solvent free. This product can be applied using standard trowels and in the same manner as standard adhesives. It provides a strong bond while remaining elastomeric to compensate for the normal expansion and contraction of wood floors.

## LEED Credits

⊞ **IEQ 4.1**
Low-Emitting Materials—
Adhesives and Sealants

**Information**
DriTac Flooring Products, LLC
60 Webro Road
Clifton, NJ 07012
T 973 614 9000
F 973 614 9099
info@dritac.com
www.dritac.com

# DuroDesign FSC Oak Flooring

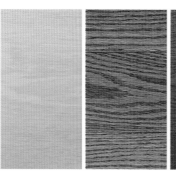  

## LEED Credits

**✛ MR 7**
Certified Wood

**⊞ IEQ 4.1**
Low-Emitting Materials—
Adhesives and Sealants

### Information
DuroDesign Flooring, Inc.
4656 Louis B. Mayer Street
Unit #9
Laval, QC H7P 6E4
Canada
T 450 978 3403
F 450 978 2542
info@durodesign.com
www.durodesign.com

### What is it?
Oak flooring harvested using sustainable methods

### Where can I use it?
Flooring

### Why is it green?
Oak makes for beautiful flooring, but it has a harvest cycle that can be around 60 years—it can easily be overlogged, destroying forests much faster than they can be replenished. DuroDesign sources oak from FSC-certified forests, which means that the wood is being harvested in a sustainable manner that minimizes the negative impact on the growth of the particular wood species. There is also an unprecedented level of accountability, as every FSC-certified material must have its identifier number on it or its packaging, which indicates the chain of custody from its source. In addition, the company uses a polyurethane finishing system that contains very low levels of VOCs.

### Special Considerations
*FSC-certified wood must account for 50 percent of all wood materials to qualify for credit.*

# GeoDeck

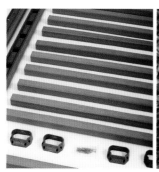

### What is it?
Composite decking and railing system

### Where can I use it?
Outdoors decks

### Why is it green?
GeoDeck is a decking and railing system made from a mix of recycled materials, including polyethylene and cellulose fiber, as well as calcium carbonate and clay. It comes in standard wood finishes and can be cut, milled, drilled, and fastened like any ordinary decking material. Its light weight makes it easier to work with and cuts down on transportation costs. A material made mostly from recycled content, GeoDeck is easily recyclable with general construction debris—things that are made from recycled content can easily be recycled again.

### Special Considerations
*A lighter color will absorb less heat and possibly make the deck area more comfortable.*

## LEED Credits

**✦ MR 2**
Construction Waste
Management

**✦ MR 4**
Recycled Content

### Information
GeoDeck
1518 South Broadway
Green Bay, WI 54304
T 877 804 0137
info@geodeck.com
www.geodeck.com

# i-plas

## LEED Credits

---

**+ MR 2**
Construction Waste
Management

**+ MR 4**
Recycled Content

---

### Information
i-plas
Ridings Business Park
Hopwood Lane
Halifax, West Yorkshire
HX1 3TT
United Kingdom
T +44 1422 350816
F +44 1422 347524
sales@i-plas.co.uk
www.i-plas.co.uk

### What is it?
Plastic lumber

### Where can I use it?
Outdoor furniture, boardwalks, ground protection,
in place of lumber

### Why is it green?
The UK-based company i-plas makes lumber products
from 100 percent recycled and recyclable plastics that would
otherwise find their way to a landfill. Plastic lumber offers
several advantages over standard timber products. According
to the company, it lasts five times longer and is rot-, algae-,
chip-, splinter-, crack-, insect-, and rodent-proof, making it
a maintenance-free option. It can be worked with and installed
just like standard lumber and will hold nails and screws just
as well.

### Special Considerations
*At the time of this writing, the company had not yet established
global distribution.*

# Kirei Bamboo

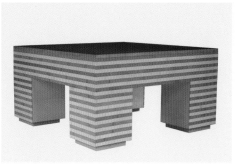

**What is it?**
Surface material made from bamboo

**Where can I use it?**
Walls, flooring, furniture, cabinetry

**Why is it green?**
Kirei uses Moso bamboo, one of the fastest growing bamboo plants in the world, capable of growing a foot each day, to create surface materials. The bamboo is harvested and made into strips, which are then bonded together and laminated using low-VOC adhesives and binders with no added urea formaldehyde.

Bamboo has the characteristics of many hardwoods and is just as durable. It can be used in the same applications as standard wood products, and there is no need to worry about toxic off-gassing.

**Special Considerations**
*Kirei is currently in the process of obtaining FSC-certification for its entire supply chain to make this material qualify for the Certified Wood credit.*

## LEED Credits

✦ **MR 6**
Rapidly Renewable Materials

⊞ **IEQ 4.4**
Low-Emitting Materials—
Composite Wood and
Agrifiber Products

**Information**
Kirei USA
412 North Cedros Avenue
Solana Beach, CA 92075
T 619 236 9924
F 240 220 5946
info@kireiusa.com
www.kireiusa.com

# Kirei Board

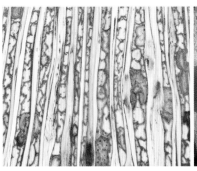  

## LEED Credits

**+ MR 4**
Recycled Content

**+ MR 6**
Rapidly Renewable Materials

**⊞ IEQ 4.4**
Low-Emitting Materials—
Composite Wood and
Agrifiber Products

### Information
Kirei USA
412 North Cedros Avenue
Solana Beach, CA 92075
T 619 236 9924
F 240 220 5946
info@kireiusa.com
www.kireiusa.com

**What is it?**
Environmentally friendly finishing material

**Where can I use it?**
Flooring, cabinetry, furniture

**Why is it green?**
Kirei Board is made from sorghum straw and is a great
alternative to other wood products. Sorghum stalks are the
waste product left after the usable parts of the plant (used as
feed) are harvested. These stalks would normally be taken
to a landfill or burned. This produces a uniquely eco-sensitive
building product; not only is it a rapidly renewable resource,
since it is harvested on an annual basis, but turning the
discarded stalks into a building material makes it recycled
content as well.

Sorghum straw makes up 90 percent of Kirei Board. The
material is bonded together using a nontoxic adhesive that
does not include any added urea formaldehyde, and they also
use a water-based adhesive, KR Bond, to finish the boards.
They can be cut, nailed, or screwed just like standard wood
panels. Since it is a finished material, no further painting or
design elements are needed once installed.

# Kirei Wheatboard

### What is it?
Medium-density fiberboard (MDF) made from discarded wheat stalks

### Where can I use it?
Walls, flooring, furniture, cabinetry

### Why is it green?
Kirei takes the wheat stalks left over after annual wheat harvests from all over the world, which would ordinarily go to landfills, and recycles them into a healthy alternative to standard MDF. After the stalks are ground up, they are bonded together using zero-VOC adhesives and no added urea formaldehyde. That means that no toxic formaldehyde will be released into the air each time a cut is made. In addition, it can be used as a finished product and does not require added paints or coverings.

## LEED Credits

+ **MR 4**
Recycled Content

+ **MR 6**
Rapidly Renewable Materials

⊞ **IEQ 4.4**
Low-Emitting Materials—Composite Wood and Agrifiber Products

### Information
Kirei USA
412 North Cedros Avenue
Solana Beach, CA 92075
T 619 236 9924
F 240 220 5946
info@kireiusa.com
www.kireiusa.com

# Natural Fiber Boards

## LEED Credits

**+ MR 4**
Recycled Content

**+ MR 6**
Rapidly Renewable Materials

**⊞ IEQ 4.4**
Low-Emitting Materials—
Composite Wood and
Agrifiber Products

### Information

Golden Vetiver Grass Board
Industry
55/121 Soi 76/1 Ekkachai Road
Bangbon Bangkok
10150
Thailand
T +662 500 5899
F +662 415 9201
marketing@golden-board.com
parinda@golden-board.com
www.golden-board.com

**What is it?**
Composite panels made from renewable and
recycled materials

**Where can I use it?**
Flooring, wall coverings, furniture, partitions, countertops

**Why is it green?**
Golden Vetiver Grass Board Industry, based in Thailand, uses
locally sourced waste products to produce environmentally
friendly wood-panel alternatives. They have several products
made up of mangosteen peels, orange peels, lemongrass,
wood chips, rice hulls, and vetiver grass.

The company grinds these up and binds them with a
nontoxic polymeric diphenylmethane diisocyanate adhesive
(pMDI). The result is a building panel that can be cut and
fastened using standard tools and maintains the character and
appearance of the materials it is made of. Making a countertop
out of orange peels or rice hulls adds contextual character to a
room that stone or composite products can't compete with.

# The Natural Glue

**What is it?**
A nontoxic adhesive made from food products

**Where can I use it?**
Wood flooring

**Why is it green?**
The Natural Glue is produced entirely from food products, mainly rice, and is an excellent wood-flooring adhesive. There are no synthetic resins or dangerous solvents or additives, so this glue will not produce any harmful off-gassing. It is astonishing that any adhesives are made from harmful compounds when it is possible to make a glue using such a naturally abundant resource.

**Special Considerations**
*This adhesive is great for flooring but may not work as well on vertical applications.*

## LEED Credits

⊞ **IEQ 4.1**
Low-Emitting Materials—
Adhesives and Sealants

**Information**
Yoshi Development New York (YDNY)
57 East 11th Street
3rd Floor
New York, NY 10003
T 212 228 0223
F 212 505 3158
yoshi@ydny.com
www.ydny.com

# Parador ClickBoard

## LEED Credits

⊞ **IEQ 4.4**
Low-Emitting Materials—
Composite Wood and
Agrifiber Products

✳ **ID 1**
Innovation in Design

### Information
Parador GmbH & Co. KG
Millenkamp 7-8
48653 Coesfeld
Germany
info@parador.de
www.parador.de

**What is it?**
Click-together paneling system

**Where can I use it?**
Walls, ceilings, floors

**Why is it green?**
Parador ClickBoard is a paneling system that snaps together like a floating glueless floor system, and it can be used on walls and ceilings as well. ClickBoard comes in a variety of finishes from stucco to natural wood veneers, which can be quickly and easily put together as a finished surface.

The boards have no added urea formaldehyde, so they qualify for the Low-Emitting Materials credit. Furthermore, each panel is coated at the factory using the company's ProAir-System, which is based on a naturally occurring protein called protectin that neutralizes pollutants. The coating will permanently absorb, degrade, and neutralize airborne pollutants, such as formaldehyde, and even bad odors from cigarette smoke or pets. Since it constantly improves the indoor air quality of a space, this finish helps qualify for an Innovation credit.

# Pioneer Millworks Engineered Flooring

**What is it?**
Engineered wood flooring

**Where can I use it?**
Flooring

**Why is it green?**
Often, engineered wood products are not considered green because they usually consist of a layer of real wood laminated to a variety of base materials using very toxic glues. Pioneer Millworks, already in the business of reclaiming wood, takes a different approach. Its engineered flooring consists of a 0.18 inch (4 mm) layer of reclaimed wood on top of FSC-certified plywood, all put together with low-VOC glue.

**Special Considerations**
*Fifty percent of all wood products used in a project must be FSC-certified in order to qualify for LEED credit.*

## LEED Credits

✦ **MR 3**
Materials Reuse

✦ **MR 7**
Certified Wood

⊞ **IEQ 4.4**
Low-Emitting Materials—
Composite Wood and
Agrifiber Products

**Information**
Pioneer Millworks Eastern Office
1180 Commercial Drive
Farmington, NY 14425
T 585 924 9970
F 585 924 9962
myfloorsrock@
pioneermillworks.com
www.pioneermillworks.com

# Plyboo Bamboo Flooring

## LEED Credits

**✦ MR 6**
Rapidly Renewable Materials

**✦ MR 7**
Certified Wood

**⊞ IEQ 4.4**
Low-Emitting Materials—
Composite Wood and
Agrifiber Products

### Information
Smith & Fong Co.
475 6th Street
San Francisco, CA 94103
T  415 896 0577
F  415 896 0583
sales@plyboo.com
www.plyboo.com

### What is it?
Flooring made from bamboo

### Where can I use it?
Flooring, paneling

### Why is it green?
Bamboo grows abundantly and quickly, and it's a sturdy and consistent building material, which makes it perfect for flooring. Smith & Fong produces Plyboo flooring from 100 percent rapidly renewable bamboo harvested from FSC-certified forests, and stringent sustainable forestry guidelines are followed. The boards also are made with no added urea formaldehyde so they don't produce harmful off-gassing and therefore qualify for the Low-Emitting Materials credit. The material can be cut and installed just like standard hardwood flooring products.

### Special Considerations
*There will be some variation in the appearance of this material, due to the nature of the material.*

# PolyWhey Natural Wood Finish

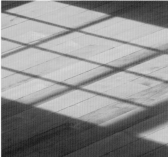

**What is it?**

Nontoxic wood finish

**Where can I use it?**

Wood floors, wood furniture

**Why is it green?**

PolyWhey is a wood finish that is easy to apply and that dries quickly. It has less than 180 g/L VOCs, making it compliant the Low-Emitting Materials (sealant) credit. When working with sealants and adhesives, it is usually a good idea to wear breathing protection. However, no protection is necessary with this sealant since it contains such a small amount of VOCs. Vermont Natural Coatings decided to go that extra step and make their cans from postconsumer recycled materials; they can be easily recycled when they are emptied, which contributes to the Construction Waste Management credit.

## LEED Credits

**+ MR 2**

Construction Waste Management

**⊞ IEQ 4.1**

Low-Emitting Materials— Adhesives and Sealants

**Information**

Vermont Natural Coatings
180 Junction Road
Hardwick, VT 05843
T 802 472 8700
F 802 472 5227
www.vermontnatural
coatings.com

# PureBond

## LEED Credits

⊞ **IEQ 4.4**
Low-Emitting Materials—
Composite Wood and
Agrifiber Products

**Information**
Columbia Forest Products
T  800 237 2428
www.columbiaforest
products.com

**What is it?**
Formaldehyde-free hardwood flooring

**Where can I use it?**
Flooring, cabinets, wall coverings

**Why is it green?**
Columbia Forest Products manufactures all of its hardwood
plywood and particleboard materials using a proprietary
process called PureBond. Using a soy-based resin binder for
structure and water resistance, the company has been able to
completely remove any formaldehyde from the manufacturing
process. This is incredibly beneficial to both people and the
natural environment since most products of these nature are
cut, drilled, and sanded, which produces particulates that
people breathe in. With these materials the only by-products
will be completely natural and nontoxic.

**Special Considerations**
*Proper eye and lung protection should still be used to avoid
inhaling wood fibers.*

# Reclaimed Indonesian Hardwood

### What is it?
Aged hardwood reclaimed from Indonesia

### Where can I use it?
Beams, flooring, furniture, sculptural elements

### Why is it green?
All of San Juan Ventures' FSC-certified reclaimed wood is sourced from native Indonesian structures called *joglos* and from abandoned factories that used wood for supports and foundations. They also get ulin, or ironwood, from boat beams and utility poles.

The aptness of the name *ironwood* is apparent as soon as it is picked up. A section about the size of a bowling ball weighed over 25 pounds. San Juan works with locals to source the wood in order to respect the potential and beauty of these specimens. This material is exceptionally beautiful and conveys a history that modern materials cannot.

### Special Considerations
*Fifty percent of all wood products used in a project must be FSC certified in order to qualify for LEED credit.*

## LEED Credits

**+ MR 3**
Materials Reuse

**+ MR 7**
Certified Wood

### Information
San Juan Ventures
P.O. Box 471
Lake Forest, IL 60042
F 847 234 2832

# Rubio Monocoat Oil Plus

## LEED Credits

### ⊞ IEQ 4.2
Low-Emitting Materials—
Paints and Coatings

### Information
Special Hardwood Products Inc.
2211 Lithonia Industrial
Boulevard
Lithonia, GA 30058
T 877 928 9663
sales@specialhardwood.com
info@monocoat.us
www.specialhardwood.com

**What is it?**
Nontoxic wood sealant

**Where can I use it?**
Flooring

**Why is it green?**
Rubio Monocoat Oil Plus forms a long-lasting, durable, molecular-level bond with wood fibers. It comes in forty standard tints and can be applied without any special skills. It contains no VOCs and is water and heat resistant, making it ideals for kitchens or bathrooms. This natural vegetable oil forms such a complete bond (in only 15 seconds) with the wood that a second coat is unnecessary. This eliminates the need for overlapping brush strokes (since the additional coat would just wash off), or different saturation levels and tints.

**Special Considerations**
*When preparing a submittal for the Low-Emitting Materials credit, you must provide the product name, VOC levels, and source of that information.*

# Sunflower Seed Board

**What is it?**
Boards made from sunflower seed hulls

**Where can I use it?**
Cabinetry, furniture, wall coverings

**Why is it green?**
Sunflower seed hulls can be turned—without the addition of any urea formaldehyde—into an agrifiber board that can be worked with using typical carpentry tools. The seed hulls are a rapidly renewable resource, and because the hulls would otherwise be discarded, it is also considered a recycled material. In addition, all materials are sourced from within 500 miles of the company's facility in Byron Center, Michigan. The texture of the raw resource is visible in this material, making it a nice choice for a green building project.

## LEED Credits

**+ MR 4**
Recycled Content

**+ MR 5**
Regional Materials

**+ MR 6**
Rapidly Renewable Materials

**⊞ IEQ 4.4**
Low-Emitting Materials—
Composite Wood and
Agrifiber Products

**Information**
VanBeek's Custom
Wood Products
7950 Clyde Park Avenue SW
Byron Center, MI 49315
T 616 583 9002
F 616 583 9004
info@vanbeekscwp.com
www.vanbeekscwp.com

# Terramica

## LEED Credits

**✛ MR 4**
Recycled Content

**✛ MR 5**
Regional Materials

**⊞ IEQ 4.4**
Low-Emitting Materials—
Composite Wood and
Agrifiber Products

### Information
Potlatch Corporation
601 West First Avenue
Suite 1600
Spokane, WA 99201
T 509 835 1500
www.potlatchcorp.com

### What is it?
Particleboard

### Where can I use it?
Furniture, cabinetry, shelving, countertops, wall coverings

### Why is it green?
Particleboard is a cheap alternative to solid paneling, but it has historically not been very green because the particles are often bonded together using the cheapest possible agent, urea formaldehyde. Terramica is made from 100 percent preconsumer recycled content and contains no added urea formaldehyde. Third-party tests have confirmed that the level of formaldehyde in this material is so low that it is similar to the level found in nature. The scraps that make up Terramica come from white wood species like Douglas fir and pine, and it can be manipulated using standard carpentry tools and skills. All materials are sourced locally to the manufacturing facility in Post Falls, Idaho, so a project that uses Terramica will qualify for Regional Materials credit if located within 500 miles.

### Special Considerations
*While urea formaldehyde is strictly forbidden in green buildings, phenol formaldehyde is acceptable.*

# Timbron

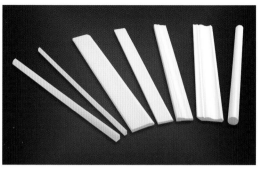  

### What is it?

Moldings made of 100 percent recycled material

### Where can I use it?

Baseboards, crown moldings, kitchen islands

### Why is it green?

Timbron moldings are made from 85 percent post-consumer and 15 percent preconsumer content, which is sourced primarily from polystyrene packaging. They can be cut and manipulated like regular moldings, and come in several different styles. All of the source materials are procured locally, so if the project is located within 500 miles of Stockton, California, this product also qualifies for the Regional Materials credit. The material is completely recyclable, extremely durable, waterproof, and pest proof, and the manufacturing process uses no VOCs, so there's no concern of off-gassing.

### Special Considerations

*When calculating recycled content, remember that preconsumer counts for half as much as postconsumer, so if there is a mix of the two in a single product, you must make the appropriate calculations.*

## LEED Credits

✦ **MR 2**
Construction Waste
Management

✦ **MR 4**
Recycled Content

✦ **MR 5**
Regional Materials

### Information

Timbron International, Inc.
1333 North California
Boulevard
Suite 545
Walnut Creek, CA 94596
T 925 943 1632
F 925 943 1164
www.timbron.com

# Vintage Barrel Collection

## LEED Credits

**+ MR 3**

Materials Reuse

### Information

Fontenay Woods

Kate Reidel

T 714 345 6739 / 800 651 8225

info@fontenaywood.com

www.fontenaywood.com

**What is it?**

Reclaimed-wood finish

**Where can I use it?**

Flooring, furniture, wall coverings

**Why is it green?**

Fontenay Woods acquires vintage wine barrels from vineyards and turns them into a unique finishing product—primarily for use as flooring. Each piece of wood is slightly different because of the way the wine it houses stained it. On some sections burned-in words that identify the vintner or year of production are visible—there is history in every piece. The most obvious use for this material would be the floor of a wine cellar, but it can be used as a finish material on furniture, ceiling paneling, a countertop surface, or in place of wall panels.

**Special Considerations**

*Different pieces of wood may vary greatly in appearance from each other, which can produce a nice overall effect.*

# World Mix Flooring

**What is it?**
Reclaimed-wood flooring

**Where can I use it?**
Flooring

**Why is it green?**
Most of the large shipping crates used in the United States are made from pine, one of the cheapest and most durable woods available in the United States. But this is not the case in other countries. Lumber that we consider exotic and interesting, like ulin or eucalyptus, are other countries' version of pine. TerraMai has a long history of creating sustainable products, and it continues the tradition with World Mix flooring. It reclaims wood from shipping crates around the world, which is generally chosen for its durability (based on both the strength of the individual pieces and the species of wood), making the material excellent for flooring. Among the species found in this flooring are balau, mempening, bintangor, agoho, mertas, and thitka, resulting in reds, rich browns, and light blonds.

## LEED Credits

✦ **MR 3**
Materials Reuse

**Information**
TerraMai
205 North Mt. Shasta Boulevard
Suite 500
Mount Shasta, CA 96067
T  530 926 6100 / 800 220 9062
F  530 926 6126
info@terramai.com
www.terramai.com

# 3

# THERMAL & MOISTURE PROTECTION

# Agriboard

## LEED Credits

* **EA P2**
Minimum Energy Performance

* **EA 1**
Optimize Energy Performance

+ **MR 2**
Construction Waste Management

+ **MR 5**
Regional Materials

+ **MR 6**
Rapidly Renewable Materials

⊞ **IEQ 4.4**
Low-Emitting Materials—Composite Wood and Agrifiber Products

### Information

Agriboard Industries
Ryan Development Company, LC
8301 East 21st Street North
Suite 320
Wichita, KS 67206
T 316 630 9223 / 866 247 4267
F 316 636 9255
sales@agriboard.com
www.agriboard.com

**What is it?**
Prefabricated building-panel system made from renewable materials

**Where can I use it?**
Walls, floors, roofs

**Why is it green?**
Agriboard Industries uses high pressure, instead of chemical additives or formaldehyde binders, to compress rapidly renewable straw into a solid thermal mass. This core is then laminated on both sides with a sheet of OSB. The resulting panels allow virtually no air leakage, and they can provide a thermal resistance of R-25.4, much higher than standard framing. These panels can be load bearing and work equally well for residential and commercial applications. The panels are designed at the factory, where all door and window openings, as well as mechanical and HVAC penetrations, are calculated and cut. This allows a structure to be built many times faster than with traditional framing—the company was able to construct a 50,000-square-foot post office in one week—since a portion of the construction is done before the material arrives, and this process also produces a significant reduction in waste. Since all of the materials for these panels are manufactured using local straw within 500 miles of Wichita, Kansas, they will qualify for a Regional Materials credit.

# Astra-Glaze-SW+

**What is it?**
Concrete masonry unit with a permanently bonded finished facing

**Where can I use it?**
Structural walls, interior finish walls

**Why is it green?**
Astra-Glaze-SW+ saves a lot of time and labor because there is no need to apply a finish after a mason installs these units as with a regular concrete-block wall. With this material you don't need to involve a different trade to apply a stucco finish or hang and paint drywall. These blocks have a thermoset glazing that has been baked onto them, and they contain 38 percent preconsumer recycled content. All materials are extracted regionally, so a project within 500 miles of the factories in Emigsville, Pennsylvania; Morris, Illinois; or Phoenix, Arizona, will likely qualify for the Regional Materials credit. The concrete in these units has a high thermal mass to help optimize energy usage, and it also provides a 4-hour fire rating. They are easy to clean and maintain and are available in dozens of different finished colors and textures.

## LEED Credits

* **EA P2**
Minimum Energy Performance

* **EA 1**
Optimize Energy Performance

+ **MR 4**
Recycled Content

+ **MR 5**
Regional Materials

**Information**
Trenwyth Industries
One Connelly Road
Emigsville, PA 17318
T 800 233 1924
F 717 764 6774
www.trenwyth.com

# BioBased Insulation

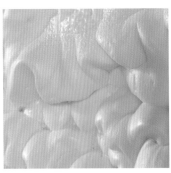   

## LEED Credits

* **EA P2**
Minimum Energy Performance

* **EA 1**
Optimize Energy Performance

+ **MR 6**
Rapidly Renewable Materials

### Information

BioBased Insulation
1475 West Cato Springs Road
Fayetteville, AR 72701
T  479 966 4600
F  479 966 4601
info@biobased.net
www.biobased.net

### What is it?
Soy-based spray-in foam insulation

### Where can I use it?
Inside walls, attic, floors, spot insulating

### Why is it green?
BioBased Insulation is a soy-based polyurethane insulation. Spray-in insulation has several advantages over other forms. It fills in every crack and crevice as it expands when injected into the space—this can greatly reduce or even completely eliminate the air gaps that allow heat to escape or cold air to enter a space. In addition, spray-in insulation maintains its thermal and acoustical insulating value in perpetuity—it expands and hardens to create a protective barrier—unlike other forms whose performance will degrade over time. Also, since this insulation comes from a soy base, it is considered a rapidly renewable material.

### Special Considerations
*Foam insulation tends to be significantly more expensive than traditional insulating methods; however, it does provide superior performance in the long term. It's easiest to justify this added cost in a home.*

# COOLWALL

### What is it?
Insulating exterior paint

### Where can I use it?
Exterior walls

### Why is it green?
COOLWALL from Textured Coatings of America can reduce the temperature of your exterior walls by around 40 degrees. It is applied like regular paint, requiring no special skills. It uses a proprietary formula that changes the invisible portion of the light spectrum to reflect solar energy, making the surface reflective and lowering the surface temperature and consequently the interior temperature. This cooling provides significant energy savings.

### Special Considerations
*Must be applied evenly and completely to achieve the best results.*

## LEED Credits

--------------------------------------------

✳ **EA P2**
Minimum Energy Performance

✳ **EA 1**
Optimize Energy Performance

---

### Information
Textured Coatings of America, Inc.
2422 East 15th Street
Panama City, FL 32405
T  800 454 0340
F  850 913 8619
info@texcote.com
www.texcote.com

# EcoClad

## LEED Credits

+ **MR 2**
Construction Waste
Management

+ **MR 4**
Recycled Content

+ **MR 5**
Regional Materials

+ **MR 7**
Certified Wood

⊞ **IEQ 4.1**
Low-Emitting Materials—
Adhesives and Sealants

### Information
Klip BioTechnologies, LLC
7314 Canyon Road East
Puyallup, WA 98371
T  253 507 4622
F  253 507 4623
info@kliptech.com
joel@kliptech.com
www.kliptech.com

### What is it?
Surfacing made of recycled material and certified renewable wood

### Where can I use it?
Exterior cladding, interior wall covering

### Why is it green?
EcoClad is made from FSC-certified fibers: half bamboo and half postconsumer recycled paper. Bamboo is a rapidly renewable resource, and the postconsumer recycled content means it counts for full value under the Recycled Content credit. The blend is bound together using a water-based resin that contains no solvents or VOCs. The panels can be manufactured to mimic an endless number of architectural looks, from different base colors to several natural wood grains. They have a special UV coating that guarantees they will be fade resistant for at least 10 years. They are also highly resistant to scratches and impact. They can be easily recycled, contributing less to the landfill after demolition.

# EcoRock

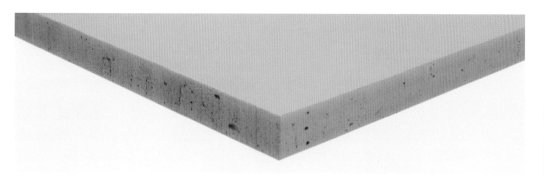

**What is it?**
Drywall made from recycled materials

**Where can I use it?**
Ceilings, walls

**Why is it green?**
EcoRock works like any drywall product and is hung in the same way, but it is easier to work with. It is made from a proprietary mix of 80 percent preconsumer recycled content—from cement and steel plants—and contains no gypsum. It requires 80 percent less energy to produce EcoRock since the boards are naturally cured and dried rather than baked in an oven. When these boards are cut, significantly less dust is released into the air because the curing process compacts them. EcoRock can be used as a pH additive for soil and is more mold-resistant than standard drywall. In addition, it is easily recycled at the end of its life: the cutoffs and scraps generated during manufacturing can be shredded and mixed to make more EcoRock.

## LEED Credits

**✦ MR 2**
Construction Waste
Management

**✦ MR 4**
Recycled Content

**✦ MR 5**
Regional Materials

**Information**
Serious Materials
1250 Elko Drive
Sunnyvale, CA 94089
T  800 797 8159
info@SeriousMaterials.com
www.seriousmaterials.com

# EcoStar Roof Tiles

## LEED Credits

+ **MR 2**
Construction Waste
Management

+ **MR 4**
Recycled Content

### Information
EcoStar, a division of
Carlisle SynTec
P.O. Box 7000
Carlisle, PA 17013
T 800 211 7170
F 888 780 9870
www.ecostar.carlisle.com

**What is it?**
Roof tiles made from recycled content

**Where can I use it?**
Roofs

**Why is it green?**
EcoStar makes roofing tiles that resemble different natural substances like slate and cedar shakes. The tiles are made with between 70 and 80 percent preconsumer recycled content. It's always interesting to discover the source of a recycled material; in this case, the raw materials come from car bumpers and the by-products of baby diaper production. The tiles provide higher impact resistance and durability then their natural equivalents.

# Glass Ore

 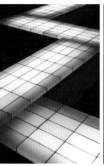  

**What is it?**
Hand-cast glass bricks

**Where can I use it?**
Walls, partitions, walkways

**Why is it green?**
Glass Ores are literally glass bricks. They allow light into a space even when a glass surface cannot be installed, and they offer structural integrity. The bricks don't allow for total light transmission, but when they are backlit they produce an absolutely stunning effect.

You can build a wall out of these and never have to turn the lights on, as long as the sun is shining. It may be difficult to demonstrate how these qualify for energy optimization, but if you don't need to turn on lights, you will save energy. The bricks can be backlit with artificial lights, and using different colors will create a range of effects.

They can also be used for walkways and lit from beneath with LED lights, creating a safely lit path with no aboveground lights and very low electrical usage.

**Special Considerations**
*These bricks may be costly, but they are well worth it for the energy savings and the unique look they offer.*

## LEED Credits

⊞ **IEQ 8.1**
Daylight and Views—Daylight

**Information**
Technical Glass Products
8107 Bracken Place SE
Snoqualmie, WA 98065
T  800 426 0279
F  800 451 9857
sales@fireglass.com
www.fireglass.com

# Green Living Wall

## LEED Credits

⊙ **SS 6.1**
Stormwater Design—
Quantity Control

⊙ **SS 6.2**
Stormwater Design—
Quality Control

⊙ **SS 7.1**
Heat Island Effect—Nonroof

✳ **EA P2**
Minimum Energy Performance

✳ **EA 1**
Optimize Energy Performance

⊞ **IEQ P1**
Minimum Indoor Air Quality
Performance

### Information
Green Living
Technologies, LLC
T  800 631 8001
F  585 467 1103
info@agreenroof.com
www.agreenroof.com

### What is it?
Vertical vegetated surface system

### Where can I use it?
Exterior walls, interior walls, freestanding units

### Why is it green?
Green Living Technologies, which specializes in green roof design, produces the Green Living Wall, a vertical application of their system. It is built on a carrier system made of recyclable aluminum that comes in sections and rests on brackets, which makes installation very simple. The metal forms of the carrier system are extremely durable and will not be bent out of shape by the weight of the planting medium, which varies depending on what you want to grow—as different species are different densities and weights. The system allows stormwater to be directed into the forms to effectively irrigate the plants—the dirt filters the water on the way to the plant. Just as green roofs eliminate the heat-island effect on horizontal surfaces, this system reduces cooling loads by protecting the structure from solar radiation.

The company also offers interior and freestanding versions of the wall. Indoors, plants clean the air, create oxygen, and provide humidity. They also offer people a psychological connection to the outdoors, improving productivity and mood and creating a healthier interior environment.

### Special Considerations
*Be sure to plant species that are suited to your particular geographic area.*

# GreenSeries

**What is it?**

Nontoxic adhesives and sealants

**Where can I use it?**

As adhesives and sealants are needed

**Why is it green?**

GreenSeries is an entire line of environmentally friendly adhesives and sealants produced by Henkel with minimal levels of VOCs, most with less than 5 g/L. The line has multipurpose adhesives for use on paneling, subflooring, and drywall and sealants that provide protection against drafts and fire and dampen sound. There is even a low-VOC version of an expanding-foam sealant, a product that is traditionally notorious for high VOC content. All of these sealants can be used to improve tightness around pipe and duct penetration. These products can seal the spots even after the building envelope has been enclosed.

**Special Considerations**

*To qualify for credit, each compound used must be properly documented.*

## LEED Credits

- - - - - - - - - - - - - - - - - - - - - - - - - - - - - - - -

✳ **EA P2**

Minimum Energy Performance

✳ **EA 1**

Optimize Energy Performance

⊞ **IEQ 4.1**

Low-Emitting Materials—
Adhesives and Sealants

**Information**

Henkel Corporation
32150 Just Imagine Drive
Avon, OH 44011
T 800 321 3578
www.greenseries.com

# holzFlex 040

## LEED Credits

✷ **EA P2**
Minimum Energy Performance

✷ **EA 1**
Optimize Energy Performance

✦ **MR 2**
Construction Waste
Management

✦ **MR 4**
Recycled Content

### Information
Ecological Building Systems
Main Street
Athboy, Meath
Ireland
T  +353 46 9432104
F  +353 46 9432435
info@ecologicalbuilding
systems.com
www.ecologicalbuilding
systems.com

**What is it?**
Slab-form insulation made from wood fiber

**Where can I use it?**
Roofs, walls, floors

**Why is it green?**
This semirigid insulation board made from recycled paper
and wood fibers has excellent thermal and acoustic insulating
properties. It is very easy to install since it can be cut and
installed using standard carpentry tools, and as it contains
no irritants, it can be handled without protective equipment.
A totally natural material, holzFlex 040 is able to absorb and
release moisture and efficiently regulate its own temperature,
making it equally effective in heating or cooling. Due to its
semirigid construction, it is ideal for placement between joists
and rafters; it will hold itself in place.

**Special Considerations**
*This insulation must be cut with a saw, unlike other forms of
insulation.*

# Igloo Cellulose Insulation

### What is it?
Cellulose insulation made from recycled materials

### Where can I use it?
Ceilings, walls

### Why is it green?
Igloo makes its cellulose insulation from 85 percent recycled wood fibers. The remaining 15 percent comes from various biodegradable materials, so the insulation can be recycled at the end of its life. The individual fibers are treated with natural additives, making the insulation fire resistant; the product also provides excellent acoustic insulation. One of the benefits to blown-in cellulose is that—like expanding spray-foam insulation—it fills in crevices around pipe or wire penetrations to provide a much more thorough seal than roll insulation. Each inch of cellulose will provide an R-value of 3.7. Eleven inches of Igloo Cellulose on top of a ceiling in the attic will achieve an effective R-value of 40.

## LEED Credits

✳ **EA P2**
Minimum Energy Performance

✳ **EA 1**
Optimize Energy Performance

✦ **MR 2**
Construction Waste Management

✦ **MR 4**
Recycled Content

### Information
Igloo Cellulose Inc.
195 Brunswick
Pointe-Claire, Québec H9R 4Z1
Canada
T 514 694 1485
F 514 694 3999
Igloo@cellulose.com
www.cellulose.com

# InSpire Wall

## LEED Credits

* **EA P2**
Minimum Energy Performance

* **EA 1**
Optimize Energy Performance

### Information
Atas Headquarters
6612 Snowdrift Road
Allentown, PA 18106
T  610 395 8445 / 800 468 1441
F  610 395 9342
www.atas.com

### What is it?
Solar-heat-collecting wall

### Where can I use it?
Exterior walls

### Why is it green?
Solar hot water heaters use the sun's energy to preheat water entering a building so the conventional water heater doesn't have to use as much energy to bring the water to the desired temperature. The InSpire wall uses the same principle, preheating air outside the building's external walls before it enters the HVAC system.

The wall is a precisely perforated metal skin mounted a few inches away from the exterior of the building. The sun heats this skin, and hot air is drawn in through the perforations, where it enters the building's air-handling systems. If the outside air is 40 degrees and the desired interior temperature is 72 degrees, a typical HVAC system would require enough energy to raise the incoming air's temperature by 32 degrees. The InSpire wall system heats the air to 60 degrees before entering the HVAC system, which will only need energy to heat the air another 12 degrees— a significant reduction in energy demand.

### Special Considerations
*Performance may vary depending on the climate where the project is located.*

# Insuladd

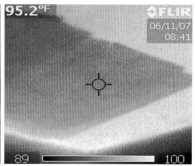

### What is it?
A paint additive that turns paint into an insulator

### Where can I use it?
Interior walls, exterior walls, roofs

### Why is it green?
Insuladd was developed in conjunction with NASA and converts any paint into a spreadable radiant barrier that will block thermal transfer. A blend of ceramic microspheres, this mixture can be added to any paint and applied anywhere to create a radiant surface. This additive helps stop the flow of heat through painted surfaces so the room can retain heat in the winter and block it in the summer. A savings of up to 20 percent on heating and cooling costs can be realized using this material. Since it is mixed in with standard paint, there is no learning curve for this product.

### Special Considerations
*Make sure the compound is mixed in thoroughly to ensure maximum effectiveness.*

## LEED Credits

* **EA P2**
Minimum Energy Performance

* **EA 1**
Optimize Energy Performance

### Information
The Insuladd Company
412 Waterside Drive
Merritt Island, FL 32952
T  321 453 5060
F  321 453 5060
sales@insuladd.com
www.insuladd.com

# LiveRoof

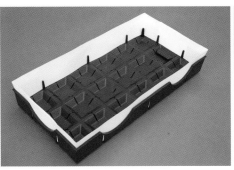 

## LEED Credits

⊙ **SS 5.1**
Site Development—
Protect or Restore Habitat

⊙ **SS 5.2**
Site Development—
Maximize Open Space

⊙ **SS 6.1**
Stormwater Design—
Quantity Control

⊙ **SS 6.2**
Stormwater Design—
Quality Control

⊙ **SS 7.1**
Heat Island Effect—Nonroof

⊙ **SS 7.2**
Heat Island Effect—Roof

💧 **WE 1**
Water Efficient Landscaping

✳ **EA P2**
Minimum Energy Performance

✳ **EA 1**
Optimize Energy Performance

✦ **MR 4**
Recycled Content

✦ **MR 5**
Regional Materials

✦ **MR 6**
Rapidly Renewable
Materials

**Information**
LiveRoof LLC
P.O. Box 533
Spring Lake, MI 49456
T 616 842 1392 / 800 875 1392
F 616 842 3273
sales@liveroof.com
www.liveroof.com

# LiveRoof

**What is it?**

Modular vegetated roof system

**Where can I use it?**

Roofs, vegetated ground areas

**Why is it green?**

LiveRoof facilitates the installation of a vegetated roof that boosts heating and cooling efficiency. It is made of modular boxes that are prefilled with the company's own growing medium and a variety of plants. When the units arrive on site, they can be placed tightly next to each other directly on the roof surface, where the plants will continue to grow.

The roof structure will need to be planned around this system because it is extensive and can weigh up to 28 pounds per square foot when saturated. The units have built-in drainage that moves excess water away from the units so that it can be recaptured and reused. Unlike other green roof systems that are not prevegetated, this system looks great the day it is installed and requires significantly less installation labor and maintenance.

A vegetated roof can reduce cooling demands by insulating a structure from thermal energy, thereby reducing energy costs. In an urban environment or a previously developed site, a green roof can provide open space usually destroyed during development. Green roofs can create a private park in the middle of a dense city for employees or residents to enjoy. The LiveRoof modules are made from 100 percent recycled polypropylene, and all materials for the carriers are sourced within fifteen miles of the company's facility in Spring Lake, Michigan.

# LUCCOtherm

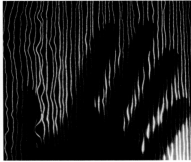

## LEED Credits

**✳ EA P2**
Minimum Energy Performance

**✳ EA 1**
Optimize Energy Performance

**⊞ IEQ 8.1**
Daylight and Views—
Daylight

### Information

Luccon
Luccon Lichtbeton GmbH,
Bundesstraße 1
Klaus/Vorarlberg A-6833
Austria
T +43 650 5789845
F +43 650 3022050
info@luccon.com
www.luccon.com

### What is it?
Light-transmitting concrete

### Where can I use it?
Facades, interior partitions, countertops, decorative panels, lighting

### Why is it green?
LUCCOtherm is a translucent, high-tensile concrete that has been saturated with optical fibers, which allows light to pass through while maintaining the structural integrity and thermal resistance of standard high-tensile concrete. The insulating factor alone helps reduce energy usage, but the introduction of natural light reduces the need for artificial lighting and, therefore, power. It also makes it possible to bring in daylight to spaces where it may not have been feasible to do so before because a window would not work for structural reasons. The material comes in standard block sizes but can be custom made to just about any size necessary.

### Special Considerations
*Although the product is incredibly distinctive, it is also expensive and may be cost-prohibitive.*

# Met-Tile

**What is it?**
Metal roof tiles

**Where can I use it?**
Roofs

**Why is it green?**
Met-Tile shingles are made from corrosion-resistant zinc-aluminum alloy coated steel. They are made completely from recycled material and are completely recyclable after their lifespan, which keeps waste out of landfills. Metal shingles offer significantly better weather and pest protection than ceramic or wooden alternatives at a fraction of the weight. Most importantly, the company uses a proprietary coating system for ten of its colors, which qualifies these tiles for Energy Star Cool Roof status by stopping the absorption of heat and increasing reflection. For every 5 percent of reflectivity added to a roof, it will be approximately 4 degrees cooler. This results in a significant reduction in cooling loads and energy demands.

**Special Considerations**
*A metal roof creates a reflection that roofs of other materials do not.*

## LEED Credits

⊙ **SS 7.2**
Heat Island Effect—Roof

✳ **EA P2**
Minimum Energy Performance

✳ **EA 1**
Optimize Energy Performance

✦ **MR 2**
Construction Waste Management

**Information**
Met-Tile
1745 E. Monticello Court
Ontario 91761
Canada
T  909 947 0311
F  909 947 1510
met-tile@met-tile.com
www.met-tile.com

# Nansulate

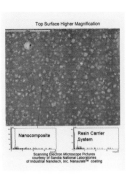

## LEED Credits

✴ **EA P2**
Minimum Energy Performance

✴ **EA 1**
Optimize Energy Performance

⊞ **IEQ 4.2**
Low-Emitting Materials—
Paints and Coatings

### Information
Industrial Nanotech, Inc.
801 Laurel Oak Drive
Suite 702
Naples, FL 34108
T 800 767 3998
F 951 324 7121
contact@nansulate.com
www.industrial-nanotech.com

### What is it?
Insulating coating

### Where can I use it?
Interior walls and ceilings, exterior wall, piping, storage tanks

### Why is it green?
Industrial Nanotech uses an insulator called Hydro-NM-Oxide, a product of nanotechnology and a poor thermal conductor, to produce Nansulate, which is an excellent insulator. Nansulate is an insulating coating made up of about 70 percent Hydro-NM-Oxide and 30 percent acrylic resin. Painting it onto a surface will result in lower thermal transfer, retaining heat during cold seasons and reflecting heat in hot seasons. The paint also contains very low amounts of VOCs, so it is safe for use indoors or in closed spaces like machine rooms.

### Special Considerations
*Make sure to apply evenly and completely to achieve maximum effectiveness.*

# Plantwall

### What is it?
Living-wall panel

### Where can I use it?
Indoor and outdoor walls

### Why is it green?
Green Fortune customizes these living wall panels to suit any application, whether an individual office, a reception area, or a building facade. The system is completely self-contained with an integrated drip-irrigation system that is automatically programmed by the company during installation.

Living walls profoundly improve the indoor environment by increasing oxygen levels and offering inhabitants a connection to the outside world. The system provides a large amount of greenery and a constantly growing and changing landscape without taking up valuable floor space.

Indoor air quality performance and a possible Innovation credit depend on the type of plant species chosen for the living wall. A plant that releases a significant amount of moisture into the air increases humidity, and a humid room feels warmer than a dry room, which reduces the need for heating and thus optimizes energy usage while improving the air quality. English ivy (*Hedera helix*) or mother-in-law's tongue (*Sansevieria trifasciata laurentii*), both of which NASA has tested and confirmed to be excellent at naturally cleaning formaldehyde, benzene, and carbon monoxide from the air, can be used to increase the chances for an Innovation credit.

### Special Considerations
*The list is long, but there are only certain kinds of species that will thrive in this type of situation, so check before you plan on using your favorite plant.*

## LEED Credits

❋ **EA P2**
Minimum Energy Performance

❋ **EA 1**
Optimize Energy Performance

⊞ **IEQ P1**
Minimum Indoor Air Quality Performance

❋ **ID 1**
Innovation in Design

### Information
Green Fortune
Stockholm, Sweden
info@greenfortune.com
www.greenfortune.com

# Reclaimed Rigid Foam Insulation

## LEED Credits

* **EA P2**
Minimum Energy Performance

* **EA 1**
Optimize Energy Performance

+ **MR 3**
Materials Reuse

### Information
Insulation Depot, Inc.
703 Waverly Street
Framingham, MA 01702
T 888 820 2760
F 508 879 9760
David@insulationdepot.com
www.insulationdepot.com

**What is it?**
Reclaimed insulation

**Where can I use it?**
Anywhere rigid foam insulation is typically used

**Why is it green?**
Insulation Depot reclaims foam insulation from hundreds of construction sites and warehouses around the country. Due to the long-lasting nature of rigid foam, the R-values of the reclaimed insulation are usually within 10 to 20 percent of their original R-value at production. The company deals primarily in EPS, XEPS, ISO, and composite foam-board insulation and has over 250 trailers full of material. Its goal is to remove one billion pounds of material from the waste stream every year and put it back to its original use in homes and commercial structures.

**Special Considerations**
*Results will vary depending on the state and age of insulation obtained.*

# Sheep Wool Insulation

### What is it?
Insulation from sheep's wool

### Where can I use it?
Walls, ceilings, attics, under flooring

### Why is it green?
The insulation, true to its name, is produced entirely from rapidly renewable sheep's wool. No additives or artificial chemicals are added—the wool is simply washed then mechanically bound without adhesives. Any waste pieces are completely biodegradable and thus do not need to go to a landfill; they can be reused or composted.

One of the problems with insulations other than mass-produced fiberglass batting is that they need chemical additives for fire protection. Wool requires no such additives for a very interesting reason; it has a very high limiting oxygen index of 25.2. For wool to burn, the oxygen content in the air must be 25.2 percent, whereas our atmosphere only contains 21 percent.

Labor costs are lower with wool insulation since it doesn't contain any irritants—it installs much faster and without any protective gear. Due to the hygroscopic nature of wool—meaning it can efficiently absorb and release ambient moisture—this product absorbs and releases moisture into the air without reducing its thermal insulating abilities.

## LEED Credits

✶ **EA P2**
Minimum Energy Performance

✶ **EA 1**
Optimize Energy Performance

✛ **MR 2**
Construction Waste Management

✛ **MR 6**
Rapidly Renewable Materials

### Information
Sheep Wool Insulation Ltd.
Unit 1, Railway Business Park
Rathdrum, Wicklow
Ireland
T +353 404 46100
F +353 404 46452
info@sheepwoolinsulation.ie
www.sheepwoolinsulation.ie

# Spaceloft

## LEED Credits

* **EA P2**
Minimum Energy Performance

* **EA 1**
Optimize Energy Performance

### Information
Aspen Aerogels, Inc.
30 Forbes Road
Building B
Northborough, MA 01532
T  508 691 1111
F  508 691 1200
www.aerogel.com

**What is it?**
Insulation made from aerogel

**Where can I use it?**
Thermal bridging, insulating floors, walls, roofs

**Why is it green?**
Aerogel, first developed in 1931, is a remarkable substance. It is often referred to as frozen smoke because it is a solid made of over 90 percent air, and it is an excellent thermal insulator. When you squeeze it, it's like squeezing a cotton ball, only it's much lighter. Since it traps air so well, it remains very thin and can provide the same insulation as something much thicker. It comes in three thicknesses, 0.1 inch (3 mm), 0.24 inch (6 mm), and 0.35 inch (9 mm). It is designed so it can be adhered to the edge of a wood or steel stud before any paneling is attached, which eliminates any thermal-bridging problems casued by gaps between the studs and finish wall surfaces. It can increase the thermal efficiency of wood studs by 15 percent and steel studs by 40 percent.

**Special Considerations**
*Aerogel-based materials can be very costly.*

# Straw Wall

### What is it?
Building panels made from straw

### Where can I use it?
Flooring, walls, roofs

### Why is it green?
When Green Design Systems set out to make a new panelized system for modular buildings, its designers decided it wasn't green enough to build a house out of panels made from rice hulls and rice straw. Once they compressed these rapidly renewable materials, they encased them with a steel mesh made from 100 percent recycled metals. They also made the frame of each panel from FSC-certified lumber. Straw has natural insulating properties and has been used as a building material for centuries.

The panels can be made in various heights, widths, and thicknesses, and can be finished using standard interior and exterior finishes like siding and drywall. They are also sturdy enough to provide structure. Any waste from installing these panels can be recycled or even composted, helping to contribute to waste management.

### Special Considerations
*Green Design Systems is a start-up company with limited production capabilities.*

## LEED Credits

✴ **EA P2**
Minimum Energy Performance

✴ **EA 1**
Optimize Energy Performance

✚ **MR 2**
Construction Waste Management

✚ **MR 4**
Recycled Content

✚ **MR 6**
Rapidly Renewable Materials

✚ **MR 7**
Certified Wood

### Information
Green Design Systems
T 707 696 2004
info@greendesignsystems.com
www.greendesignsystems.com

# Super Therm

## LEED Credits

⊙ **SS 7.2**
Heat Island Effect—Roof

✳ **EA P2**
Minimum Energy Performance

✳ **EA 1**
Optimize Energy Performance

### Information
Superior Products
International II, Inc.
10835 West 78th Street
Shawnee, KS 66214
sales@spicoatings.com
www.spicoatings.com

### What is it?
Insulating exterior coating

### Where can I use it?
Roofs, exteriors

### Why is it green?
Super Therm is an insulating coating with a ceramic base. When painted onto an exterior surface, Super Therm acts as a radiant barrier, blocking ultraviolet, visible, and infrared rays. According to the manufacturer, use of this product on a roof will produce energy savings of 20 to 70 percent and a surface temperature that is 80 degrees cooler than an untreated roof. Once applied, the coating gives the equivalent thermal ability of 6 to 8 inches of traditional insulation, blocking 95 percent of the sun's radiation and resulting in an R-value of 19.

Super Therm will last over 20 years and is an excellent option where bulky traditional insulation would restrict the flow or size of a space. For example, shipping containers have become a popular structure for building modular homes and pop-up stores, but adding rigid, foam, or batt insulation decreases precious usable space. Super Therm has been applied successfully on the exterior of these containers as the sole means of insulation.

### Special Considerations
*Must be applied evenly and completely to achieve the best results.*

# Tensotherm

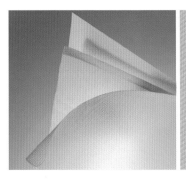

### What is it?
Efficient fabric-canopy system

### Where can I use it?
Canopies, roofs

### Why is it green?
Tensile fabric membranes are not something new; systems of cables and fabric can create a roof surface that is both flexible and easier to install than a rigid roof. Tensotherm improves on this basic design by introducing an insulated layer of Nanogel, a brand of the substance aerogel. (See also Spaceloft, page 99.) The whole Tensotherm membrane is only ½ inch thick but provides effective resistance to thermal transfer, holding in cold air in the summer and warm air in the winter. In addition, the membrane allows natural light to diffuse into a space, reducing the need for energy-demanding artificial light fixtures.

### Special Considerations
*Any fabric roof will be more susceptible to physical damage than one made out of metal or shingles.*

## LEED Credits

✴ **EA P2**
Minimum Energy Performance

✴ **EA 1**
Optimize Energy Performance

⊙ **IEQ 8.1**
Daylight and Views—
Daylight

### Information
Birdair, Inc.
65 Lawrence Bell Drive
Suite 100
Amherst, NY 14221
T  716 633 9500
F  716 633 9850
www.birdair.com

# Thermafleece

## LEED Credits

* **EA P2**
Minimum Energy Performance

* **EA 1**
Optimize Energy Performance

+ **MR 2**
Construction Waste
Management

+ **MR 6**
Rapidly Renewable Materials

### Information
Ecological Building Systems
Main Street
Athboy, Meath
Ireland
T +353 46 9432104
F +353 46 9432435
info@ecologicalbuilding
systems.com
www.ecologicalbuilding
systems.com

**What is it?**
Roll insulation made from natural wool

**Where can I use it?**
Roofs, walls, floors

**Why is it green?**
Thermafleece insulation is made from all-natural sheep's wool. This material is shaved off sheep every season without harming the animals or reducing their ability to produce more wool. Wool is one of nature's best insulators and can generate heat when it absorbs moisture from the air. Since it is a natural material, it can be installed without the use of gloves, breathing aids, or any other protective gear.

Natural derivatives are added to Thermafleece to provide insect and fire resistance. Wool is naturally breathable and hygroscopic, meaning it can efficiently absorb and release ambient moisture—it can help cool the air by releasing moisture when it's hot out and absorb moisture to help retain heat in the winter. It is easily recyclable; any waste produced during construction or demolition can be recycled as well. Finally, wool is even more efficient at cooling a space than it is at heating and can reduce the peak temperature in a building by up to 45 degrees.

# ThermaRock XI

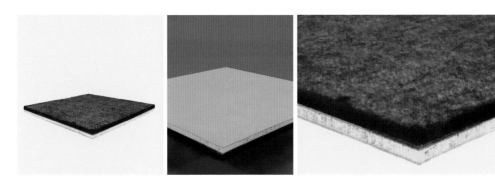

**What is it?**
Drywall with thermal-insulation properties

**Where can I use it?**
Ceilings, walls

**Why is it green?**
Standard gypsum drywall can't hold a candle to Thermarock. Actually, more accurately, it can't hold the heat of a candle compared to Thermarock. Standard drywall typically has an R-value of about 0.5. Using Thermarock increases the R-value between R-2.5 to R-4.1, dramatically improving energy efficiency and reducing heating and cooling needs. Considerably thinner widths of Thermarock can achieve the same thermal resistance as conventional drywall, minimizing the loss of floor space caused by thicker insulated walls.

**Special Considerations**
*This material will have to be worked into an energy model to accurately determine energy optimization.*

## LEED Credits

✳ **EA P2**
Minimum Energy Performance

✳ **EA 1**
Optimize Energy Performance

**Information**
Serious Materials
1250 Elko Drive
Sunnyvale, CA 94089
T  800 797 8159
info@SeriousMaterials.com
www.seriousmaterials.com

# Thermastrand

## LEED Credits

* **EA P2**
Minimum Energy Performance

* **EA 1**
Optimize Energy Performance

+ **MR 7**
Certified Wood

### Information
Ainsworth Lumber Co. Ltd.
1055 Dunsmuir Street
Suite 3194 Bentall 4
Vancouver, BC V7X 1L3
Canada
T  604 661 3200
F  604 661 3201
marketing@ainsworth.ca
www.ainsworth.ca

### What is it?
FSC-certified radiant barrier panels

### Where can I use it?
Roof insulation

### Why is it green?
These FSC-certified boards are faced with aluminum and are designed to reflect back 97 percent of radiant heat from the sun. These panels provide a barrier between the sun's heat and air-conditioned spaces, resulting in energy savings greater then 20 percent. The aluminum faces of the boards have been microperforated with thousands of tiny holes to make them breathable, helping them last longer and resist warping. They are installed easily by any roofer and are attached to the rafters before any roofing surface goes in place. Thermastrand comes in 4 x 8 foot sheets, just like standard plywood.

# Thermo-Hemp

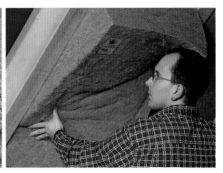

### What is it?
Mat and roll insulation made completely from hemp

### Where can I use it?
Walls, ceilings, attic space

### Why is it green?
Hemp, the world's oldest cultivated plant, has an incredibly high thermal resistance, making it an excellent insulator. It grows quickly and without the need for any herbicides or growth products, so insulation made from it is a 100 percent natural product without any additives. Since the fibers contain no proteins, Thermo-Hemp is impervious to mold growth or other infestations. It is able to absorb and release moisture without change to its insulating ability. In addition, as it contains no irritants, it requires no special protective gear to handle and install.

## LEED Credits

✽ **EA P2**
Minimum Energy Performance

✽ **EA 1**
Optimize Energy Performance

✦ **MR 6**
Rapidly Renewable Materials

### Information
Ecological Building Systems
Main Street
Athboy, Meath
Ireland
T +353 46 9432104
F +353 46-9432435
info@ecologicalbuilding
systems.com
www.ecologicalbuilding
systems.com

# THERMOMASS

## LEED Credits

* **EA P2**
Minimum Energy Performance

* **EA 1**
Optimize Energy Performance

**Information**
Composite Technologies
Corporation
1000 Technology Drive
Boone, IA 50036
T 800 232 1748
F 515 433 5074
www.thermomass.com

### What is it?
Building insulation system

### Where can I use it?
Exterior walls, foundations, floors

### Why is it green?
Most ICF systems involve a pair of Styrofoam pieces or other rigid insulation, tied together with plastic or metal ties, between which concrete is poured to form an insulated wall. THERMOMASS turns this process inside out by placing a proprietary Styrofoam closed-cell rigid insulation board between two layers of concrete.

The system integrates a series of fiber composite connectors that outperform steel rods: each connector is able to carry up to 2,500 pounds of concrete. The connections pierce the insulation board and lock into the two outer layers of concrete.

There are different theories about whether or not it's better to insulate the perimeters of a wall, which can leave a cold core. The other option is to have two cold perimeters but insulate the core, stopping thermal transfer between them. One benefit of a system like THERMOMASS is that the insulating layer is completely protected from the elements and will retain over 99 percent of its thermal resistance throughout its lifecycle.

### Special Considerations
*Some hardcore environmentalists may not like the idea of incorporating Styrofoam.*

# UltraTouch

**What is it?**

Insulation made from recycled content

**Where can I use it?**

Anywhere you use batt insulation

**Why is it green?**

UltraTouch is a superior batt insulation product using 85 percent preconsumer recycled denim and cotton fibers from denim manufacturers. This very dense material is an effective thermal and acoustic insulator, while containing no irritants or chemical additives. UltraTouch is coated with borates to act as a fire retardant, mold inhibitor, and pest repellent.

All material used in UltraTouch is sourced within 500 miles of the factory in Chandler, Arizona , which qualifies it for the Regional Materials credit. Installation is simplified with UltraTouch: it does not itch, so installers do not need to wear protective gear while handling it. Any waste pieces are easily recycled.

**Special Considerations**

*This material is very dense, and when screw-on drywall is being installed, the insulation can actually grab the screws and lock them in, which is a good thing until you want to remove them.*

## LEED Credits

✳ **EA P2**
Minimum Energy Performance

✳ **EA 1**
Optimize Energy Performance

✦ **MR 2**
Construction Waste Management

✦ **MR 4**
Recycled Content

✦ **MR 5**
Regional Materials

✦ **MR 6**
Rapidly Renewable Materials

**Information**

Bonded Logic, Inc.
24053 South Arizona Avenue
Suite 151
Chandler, AZ 85248
T 480 812 9114
F 480 812 9633
sales@bondedlogic.com
www.bondedlogic.com

# Warmcel 100

## LEED Credits

✳ **EA P2**

Minimum Energy Performance

✳ **EA 1**

Optimize Energy Performance

✦ **MR 2**

Construction Waste
Management

✦ **MR 4**

Recycled Content

### Information

Ecological Building Systems
Main Street
Athboy, Meath
Ireland
T  +353 46 9432104
F  +353 46 9432435
info@ecologicalbuilding
systems.com
www.ecologicalbuilding
systems.com

### What is it?

Cellulose insulation made from recycled content

### Where can I use it?

Anywhere you would normally use cellulose insulation

### Why is it green?

Warmcel 100 is made from 100 percent recycled newspaper. It doesn't contain any added formaldehyde and has no chlorofluorocarbons (CFCs) or VOCs. The material is easily recycled and installed. Due to the structure of cellulose insulation and its installation through a blower, which injects the material into every crevice of a space, it forms a superior seal in irregular space and around pipe and vent penetrations to give a higher-than-average thermal insulation value. With organic salts added to the recycled newspaper, Warmcel 100 is able to achieve a fire rating compliant with local codes and comparable insulations.

### Special Considerations

*While cellulose insulation gets treated to be fire retardant, many seasoned contractors shy away from it.*

# Whisper Wool

**What is it?**
Acoustic underlay

**Where can I use it?**
Under flooring

**Why is it green?**
Nature's Acoustics makes several products using sheep's wool, a rapidly renewable material that is harvested every nine to twelve months. It is completely biodegradable and has the natural ability to neutralize airborne contaminants like formaldehyde, nitrogen oxide, and sulfur dioxide.

Used as an underlayment, it is an excellent sound-dampening medium with a sound transmission class (STC) rating of 54—if a sound source is produced at a certain decibel on one side of the flooring, the result heard on the other side will be 54 decibels lower. At an STC of 54, very loud instruments and stereos are barely audible. This ⅛-inch-thick layer of wool has the equivalent sound dampening ability of a single layer of ½-inch-thick drywall glued to an 8-inch-thick concrete wall.

**Special Considerations**
*The type of underlayment you choose should depend on the type of flooring you plan on installing.*

## LEED Credits

**✦ MR 6**
Rapidly Renewable Materials

**Information**
Nature's Acoustics, Inc.
80 Old East Road
Chatsworth, GA 30705
T 706 422 8660
F 706 422 8661
info@naturesacoustics.com
www.naturesacoustics.com

# Xero Flor

## LEED Credits

⊙ **SS 5.1**
Site Development—
Protect or Restore Habitat

⊙ **SS 5.2**
Site Development—
Maximize Open Space

⊙ **SS 6.1**
Stormwater Design—
Quantity Control

⊙ **SS 6.2**
Stormwater Design—
Quality Control

⊙ **SS 7.2**
Heat Island Effect—Roof

✳ **EA P2**
Minimum Energy Performance

✳ **EA 1**
Optimize Energy Performance

✦ **MR 5**
Regional Materials

### Information
Xero Flor America, LLC
3821 East Geer Street
Durham, NC 27704
T 919 683 1073
www.xeroflora.com

**What is it?**
Pregrown green-roof system

**Where can I use it?**
Roofs

**Why is it green?**
Green roofs are one of the best things you can install on a building because they eliminate the heat-island effect, can help lower cooling costs in a building, and also filter and control the flow of stormwater that might otherwise cause soil erosion and overflow municipal water systems. Xero Flor offers an easy five-part process for installing a green roof that insures that it will function properly. First a root barrier is placed to protect the underlying roof surface, next a water-drainage mat, then a water-retention fleece that holds water to irrigate the plants, and finally the company's Xero Terr growing medium and the prevegetated sedum mat.

A vegetated roof also counts toward the credit because it restores habitats and maximizes open space. The Xero Flor system allows you to cut around paths and create an assembly space for people to use, which is especially beneficial in an urban setting. The company has several growing fields around the United States, and it is adding more, so you may be able to apply its use toward the Regional Materials credit.

**Special Considerations**
*This system will weigh between 12 and 18 pounds per square foot, and this added burden must be taken into account when the roof structure is being engineered.*

# Zalmag Shingles

**What is it?**
Stainless-steel shingles

**Where can I use it?**
Roofing, siding

**Why is it green?**
Zalmag Shingles are affordable, long-lasting stainless-steel shingles that have been galvanized with a mixture of mostly zinc, as well as aluminum and magnesium. These metal shingles give off a look that is industrial, clean, and striking. They are made from 95 percent recycled content, so they are also easily recyclable. The additional use of a cool roof coating on the shingles permits a much higher SRI and qualifies it for the Heat-Island Effect credit. This will greatly optimize energy usage and will result in savings in cooling costs of up to 15 percent or more.

## LEED Credits

⊙ **SS 7.2**
Heat Island Effect—Roof

✷ **EA P2**
Minimum Energy Performance

✷ **EA 1**
Optimize Energy Performance

✛ **MR 2**
Construction Waste Management

✛ **MR 4**
Recycled Content

**Information**
Millennium Tiles
550 East Centralia Street
Elkhorn, WI 53121
T 262 723 7778
F 262 723 7629
info@millenniumtiles.com
www.millenniumtiles.com

# 4

# DOORS & WINDOWS

# Bencore Starlight

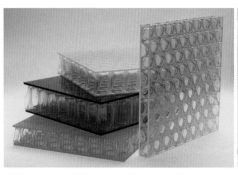  

## LEED Credits

⊞ **IEQ 8.1**
Daylight and Views—
Daylight

⊞ **IEQ 8.2**
Daylight and Views—
Views

### Information

Bencore
via S. Colombano 9
Massa Z.I. (MS) 54100
Italy
T +39 0585 830 129
F +39 0585 835 167
info@bencore.it
www.bencore.it

**What is it?**
Daylighting panels

**Where can I use it?**
Daylighting, room dividers, displays, flooring, ceilings

**Why is it green?**
Bencore Starlight panels consist of a patterned core laminated with two plastic sheets. They can help control how light enters a space. There are four different versions of the load-bearing panel; the application of a UV-protective coating on the panels can further increase the variety of applications. They work very well as room or cubicle dividers, providing privacy without limiting access to bright natural light. They also encourage more creative and efficient use of lighting within a space. For example, these panels may be used as flooring lit from below, which might eliminate the need for ceiling lights in that space.

Bencore panels come in a variety of colors and patterns, from bright cherry reds to deep navy blues. They are 40 x 120 inches in size and are available in four thicknesses, ranging from approximately ¾ inch to 1½ inches (19, 21, 34, and 36 mm).

**Special Considerations**
*Bencore products are in limited availability in the western hemisphere.*

# ClearShade IGU

### What is it?
Glass paneling

### Where can I use it?
Glass walls, daylighting, partitions

### Why is it green?
Shading devices, like awnings or shelves, help keep a space warm in the winter and cool in the summer. Because the sun is generally lower in the winter, light can pass under the shading device and into the space, warming it during the day. In the summer, when the sun is higher, the shades block a lot of the thermal energy from entering a space and help keep it cool.

ClearShade IGU panels work on a similar principle, but their function changes throughout the day rather than from season to season. Because the honeycomb cores in these panels are tubular in shape, they are transparent only when you stand right in front of them; as you move from side to side or up and down, the visible light is obscured. The same thing happens with the thermal energy from the sun. In the morning when the sun is low and directed straight at the panels, light can get in and warm the space, but as the sun reaches its peak in midday, the light is blocked since it no longer hits the panels head-on. A similar warming as in the morning happens again at the end of the day. These panels can act as a natural thermostat, allowing people to see the outdoors and light their spaces while saving energy on heating and cooling.

## LEED Credits

* **EA P2**
Minimum Energy Performance

* **EA 1**
Optimize Energy Performance

⊞ **IEQ 8.1**
Daylight and Views—
Daylight

⊞ **IEQ 8.2**
Daylight and Views—
Views

### Information
Panelite
315 West 39th Street
Studio 807
New York, NY 10018
T  212 947 8292
F  323 297 0122
info@panelite.us
www.panelite.us

# ControLite

## LEED Credits

* **EA P2**
Minimum Energy Performance

* **EA 1**
Optimize Energy Performance

⊞ **IEQ 6.1**
Controllability of Systems—
Lighting

⊞ **IEQ 6.2**
Controllability of Systems—
Thermal Comfort

⊞ **IEQ 8.1**
Daylight and Views—
Daylight

⊞ **IEQ 8.2**
Daylight and Views—
Views

### Information
CPI Daylighting Inc.
28662 North Ballard Drive
Lake Forest, IL 60045
T 847 816 1060
F 847 816 0425
info@cpidaylighting.com
www.cpidaylighting.com

**What is it?**
Light-controlling skylight system

**Where can I use it?**
Daylighting, skylights

**Why is it green?**
The system is ingenious in its simplicity. ControLite consists of polycarbonate panels with an internal layer of half-cylinder Rota-Blades, a half tube with a clear rounded side and an opaque flat side. The blades can be rotated very precisely to control the amount of light and thermal energy entering the space. Operated either manually or with a programmable automated system, these panels allow a range of between 6 percent and 60 percent of sunlight into a space. Carefully controlling light and thermal trespass can produce significant savings in heating and cooling costs. On a smaller, human scale, the system also allows individuals to control the lighting and heating of their immediate environment while still maintaining unrestricted views to the outside.

**Special Considerations**
*Unlike a static glass surface or skylight, this is a moving system that may require maintenance.*

# Translucent Polycarbonate Multi-Wall Panel Systems

### What is it?
Translucent building panels

### Where can I use it?
Urban roofs, canopies, green houses, interior partitions

### Why is it green?
Translucent Polycarbonate Multi-Wall Panel Systems is a modular panel system for creating translucent surfaces. This standing seam system—a roofing system where the individual panels are crimped together to form a seal—can be used to create entire roof structures. In places such as green houses or outdoor pools, it permits thermal energy to radiate into a space, reducing the need for artificial heating. The panel system can be used for outdoor canopies as well as interior partitions to increase light diffusion while maximizing direct views to the outside, which can improve productivity and mood. The polycarbonate used in these panels has an impact resistance 200 times greater than glass, but it only weighs 1 pound per square foot. Each side is coated with UV protection, and the panels are nontoxic and flexible enough to make curved surfaces.

### Special Considerations
*In buildings with large amounts of glass, heat gain can become an issue, and this needs to be addressed with using coatings or additional cooling systems.*

## LEED Credits

------------------------------------------

**✱ EA P2**
Minimum Energy Performance

**✱ EA 1**
Optimize Energy Performance

**⊞ IEQ 8.1**
Daylight and Views—
Daylight

**⊞ IEQ 8.2**
Daylight and Views—
Views

### Information
Co-Ex Corporation
5 Alexander Drive
Wallingford, CT 06492
T   203 679 0500 / 800 888 5364
F   203 679 0600
info@co-excorp.com
www.co-excorp.com

# 5

# FINISHES

# Alkemi

## LEED Credits

**✛ MR 4**
Recycled Content

### Information
Renewed Materials, LLC
P.O. Box 55
Cabin John, MD 20818
T   301 320 0042
F   301 320 3341
www.renewedmaterials.com

### What is it?
Surface material made from recycled content

### Where can I use it?
Countertops, tabletops, wall coverings

### Why is it green?
Alkemi is a surface material containing 35 percent preconsumer scrap metal made from fine-flake aluminum milling scraps. The shavings display their base form clearly in this product. It comes in three finishes: textured, classic, and honed, and in about a dozen different colors. Alkemi comes in thicknesses of ½ inch and ¾ inch and can be installed by any solid-surface countertop installer.

# American Clay Earth Plaster

**What is it?**
Zero-VOC coating material

**Where can I use it?**
Ceilings, walls

**Why is it green?**
American Clay Earth Plaster is an alternative to paint: it is a textured coating that makes any surface look more earthy and natural. With a variety of colors from natural pigments like ochre and selenite, Earth Plaster contains no VOCs. All of the aggregates and pigments are sourced regionally near the factory. As an added bonus, because of the dense molecular structure of the material, it produces a negative charge (and thus negative ions) when it absorbs ambient moisture. Negative ions have been linked to increases in serotonin in the brain, reducing stress and increasing energy levels.

The material ships dry to reduce waste. Once on location, it is mixed with water and troweled on like regular plaster. Any leftover material can be left to dry, and when you're ready to use it again, you simply have to break it up and add water to reuse it over and over.

**Special Considerations**
*This material is a plaster, not really a paint, so make sure the installer is familiar with plaster application.*

## LEED Credits

**+ MR 2**
Construction Waste Management

**+ MR 5**
Regional Materials

**⊞ IEQ 4.2**
Low-Emitting Materials—Paints and Coatings

**Information**
American Clay Enterprises, LLC
8724 Alameda Park Drive NE
Albuquerque, NM 87113
T 866 404 1634
F 505 244 9332
sales@americanclay.com
www.americanclay.com

# Arrowroot Grasscloth Wall Covering

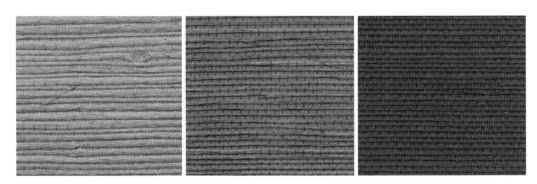

## LEED Credits

**+ MR 6**
Rapidly Renewable Materials

### Information

Cavalier Wallpapers
P.O. Box 725
Florida, NY 10921
T 800 221 5798
F 718 426 2950
customerservice@
nonwovenwallpapers.com
www.nonwovenwallpapers.com

### What is it?
Sustainable wall covering

### Where can I use it?
Walls

### Why is it green?
The Arrowroot plant was cultivated as far back as 7,000 years ago. The Arawak Indians in the Caribbean used the plant's starches as a staple of their diets, and it is believed that the name comes from its ability to draw out toxins from poison arrow wounds. Arrowroot was used for a long time to make paper until more modern and economical methods were found. As a rapidly renewable resource, it makes for a much greener alternative to standard wall coverings. It makes an excellent material for wall coverings because of its unique texture and variety of colors.

# Bark Cloth

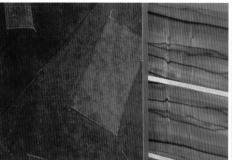

### What is it?
Natural bark laminate

### Where can I use it?
Wall coverings, room dividers, furniture coverings

### Why is it green?
Like the cork trees often used for flooring, the fig tree, or *Ficus natalensis*, regrows its bark quickly, and it is possible to remove the bark without destroying the tree. Dekodur softens the bark before sewing fragments of bark together to make larger sheets. These large pieces of cloth are bonded to high-pressure laminate sheets, which makes them durable, stain resistant, and fire resistant. The sheets make for a unique wall covering and have the appearance and texture of aged leather. They are custom made.

## LEED Credits

**+ MR 6**
Rapidly Renewable Materials

### Information
Dekodur GmbH & Co. KG
Langenthaler Str. 4 Hirschhorn
69434
Germany
T +49 6272 6890
F +49 6272 68930
info@dekodur.de
www.dekodur.de

# Bio-Glass

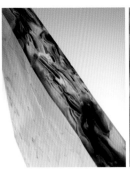 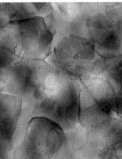 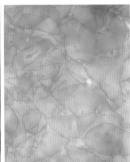 

## LEED Credits

**+ MR 2**
Construction Waste
Management

**+ MR 4**
Recycled Content

### Information

Coverings ETC
7610 NE 4th Court
Miami, FL 33138
T  305 757 6000
F  305 757 6100
info@coveringsetc.com
www.coveringsetc.com

**What is it?**
Surface material made of 100 percent recycled glass

**Where can I use it?**
Flooring, countertops, decorative surfaces

**Why is it green?**
Bio-Glass is a completely green material: it is made from 100 percent recycled material without additives or the use of any new resources in its production. The color of this material depends on the source of the glass. The lighter white and light green colors are made with glass that comes directly from factories, from glass panes broken during the manufacturing process. The darker colors—dark brown, green, and blue—come from beer and drink bottles that consumers have used and discarded. Bio-Glass creates a durable, long-lasting surface, but it can still be recycled at the end of its life and reused. When the building the product is installed in is demolished, this material can be diverted from a landfill, helping you attain the LEED credit for Construction Waste Management.

# BottleStone

**What is it?**
Surface materials made from recycled materials

**Where can I use it?**
Countertops, vanities

**Why is it green?**
BottleStone is made from 80 percent postconsumer recycled glass bottles recovered from recycling centers in the San Francisco Bay Area. The glass is ground up into $\frac{1}{8}$-inch pieces before being reconstituted using high pressure into a very strong surface. A 1-inch-thick piece of BottleStone is as strong as a $1\frac{1}{2}$-inch-thick brick and a $2\frac{1}{2}$-inch-thick concrete slab. It can be fashioned into countertops of any size and in several colors. One of the founders of BottleStone, Paul Burns, owns Fireclay Tile, a manufacturer of recycled glass tiles also featured in this book.

## LEED Credits

**+ MR 4**
Recycled Content

**Information**
Fireclay Tile
495 West Julian Street
San Jose, CA 95110
T 408 533 1226
info@bottlestone.com
www.bottlestone.com

# Carlisle Wide Plank Reclaimed Flooring

## LEED Credits

**+ MR 3**
Materials Reuse

### Information
Carlisle Wide Plank Floor
T 800 595 9663
www.wideplankflooring.com

**What is it?**
Reclaimed antique flooring

**Where can I use it?**
Flooring

**Why is it green?**
Carlisle salvages most of its eastern white pine and oak flooring from factories and textile mills in the New England area. Most of the trees of these species don't have a chance to grow fully due to overlogging, which often results in forests being leveled rapidly, before trees reach maturity. Since most hardwoods have harvest cycles that can be many decades long—oak's is about sixty years—floorboards over 6 inches wide can usually only be acquired from reclaimed sources. These boards, a part of the Carlisle Wide Plank Flooring line, offer a unique look with some history, and make a large room look that much more impressive.

# Cork Tile

### What is it?
Tile made from cork

### Where can I use it?
Walls, floors, backsplashes

### Why is it green?
Modwalls sources cork from the cork-stopper-manufacturing industry. The small circles in the tile are cut from the coin-sized pieces of stopper, which would have gone into the waste stream, making them a preconsumer recycled material. Cork is a rapidly renewable resource since cork bark can be harvested every 7 years, and it is removed from the tree without killing it. The tiles come in 1-square-foot pieces and are water-proof, making them suitable for kitchen or bathroom uses. They need to be sealed before installation for the cork to maintain its natural color.

### Special Considerations
*Due to the nature of the material, variations in appearance will occur.*

## LEED Credits

**+ MR 4**
Recycled Content

**+ MR 6**
Rapidly Renewable Materials

### Information
Modwalls
54 Old El Pueblo Road
Suite C
Scotts Valley, CA 95066
T  831 439 9734
F  831 439 9521
sales@modwalls.com
www.modwalls.com

# Debris Series

## LEED Credits

**+ MR 4**
Recycled Content

**+ MR 5**
Regional Materials

### Information
Fireclay Tile Inc.
495 West Julian Street
San Jose, CA 95110
T 408 275 1182
F 408 275 1187
info@fireclaytile.com
www.fireclaytile.com

**What is it?**
Tiles made with recycled glass

**Where can I use it?**
Floors, walls, backsplashes

**Why is it green?**
Fireclay Tile company takes waste from local gravel, asphalt, and cement production at a facility in San Francisco and mixes it with postconsumer recycled glass bottles. The result is a glass tile with about 26 percent preconsumer and 26 percent postconsumer recycled content. The company glazes its tiles in 136 colors, and each of the glazes is completely lead-free.

# Devine Color Paint

**What is it?**

Extremely low-VOC paint

**Where can I use it?**

Interiors

**Why is it green?**

Usually people complain that low-VOC paint does not coat or spread well. Devine Color has created what it calls *yogurt paint*, with the feel and consistency of thick yogurt. It spreads well without dripping and requires only one coat. The best part is that it is 99.99 percent VOC-free. To meet the Low-Emitting Materials requirement, paint must have less than 50 g/L of VOCs. Devine Color paints have about 5 g/L.

## LEED Credits

⊞ **IEQ 4.2**

Low-Emitting Materials—
Paints and Coatings

**Information**

Devine Color
668 McVey #81
Lake Oswego, OR 97034
T 503 387 5840
F 503 387 5870
contact@devinecolor.com
www.devinecolor.com

# Earth Weave

 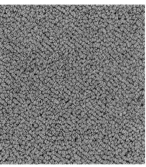 

## LEED Credits

**+ MR 2**
Construction Waste
Management

**+ MR 6**
Rapidly Renewable Materials

### Information
Earth Weave Carpet Mills, Inc.
P.O. Box 6120
Dalton, GA 30722
T  706 278 8200
F  706 278 8201
earthweave@earthweave.com
www.earthweave.com

**What is it?**
Carpet made from natural raw and rapidly renewable
materials

**Where can I use it?**
Anywhere you would use traditional carpeting

**Why is it green?**
All of Earth Weave Carpet Mills' carpets, which are Green
Label Plus certified, are made primarily with wool. A
mechanical stitching process intertwines cotton and hemp
fibers into the wool, and a nontoxic adhesive derived from
the rubber tree is used to adhere the mesh to a jute backing.
Jute is a soft vegetable fiber made up of plant cellulose that
is second only to cotton in its global production volume.
All of these materials are rapidly renewable and biodegradable, which help earn the Construction Waste Management
credit, since these carpets would break down in a standard
compost.

**Special Considerations**
*If the carpet is Green Label Plus certified, it counts no matter
how much is used.*

# EcoDomo Recycled Leather Tiles

**What is it?**
Floor and wall tiles made from recycled leather scraps

**Where can I use it?**
Floors, wall coverings

**Why is it green?**
These tiles are made of a minimum of 65 percent preconsumer recycled material taken mainly from furniture and shoe factories. The shreds of leather from this process are reassembled into tiles using rapidly renewable natural latex and rubber. Even though preconsumer content only counts for half, that's still 32.5 percent in this case, which is well over the 20 percent threshold needed to get two points for the Recycled Content credit.

## LEED Credits

✛ **MR 4**
Recycled Content

✛ **MR 6**
Rapidly Renewable Materials

**Information**
EcoDomo, LLC
14650 F Rothgeb Drive
Rockville, MD 20850
T  301 424 7717
F  301 424 7719
christian@ecodomo.com
www.ecodomo.com

# ECOmax

## LEED Credits

⊙ **SS 6.1**
Stormwater Design—
Quantity Control

✛ **MR 2**
Construction Waste
Management

✛ **MR 4**
Recycled Content

✛ **MR 5**
Regional Materials

⊞ **IEQ 4.1**
Low-Emitting Materials—
Adhesives and Sealants

**Information**
ECOsurfaces Commercial
Flooring
c/o Gerbert Limited
119 South Tree Drive
Lancaster, PA 17603
T 877 326 7873
F 717 394 1937
info@ecosurfaces.com
www.ecosurfaces.com

**What is it?**
Rubber flooring tiles

**Where can I use it?**
Flooring, decking

**Why is it green?**
ECOmax rubber flooring tiles are made almost completely from rubber taken from postconsumer recycled rubber tires and by-products of rubber roofing manufacturing. ECOsurfaces recommends using its E-Grip III adhesive, which is VOC compliant and trowels onto your base surface with ease. The floor tiles, which are recommended for both indoor or outdoor use, are molded with little feet at regular intervals that raise the tiles slightly off the subfloor or ground they are laid on. For outdoor applications, the separation between the tiles and these feet creates natural channels to allow stormwater to quickly and easily drain through and either be recaptured or percolate into the ground.

All materials are sourced and manufactured in Lancaster, Pennsylvania. Projects located anywhere in the Northeastern United States will qualify for the Regional Materials credit.

**Special Considerations**
*When these are used in a stormwater management application, the underlying surface must be properly pitched to direct the water.*

# EcoTop

### What is it?
Countertop surface made from rapidly renewable wood and recycled paper

### Where can I use it?
Countertops, vanities, floors, walls

### Why is it green?
EcoTop is made from a mixture of FSC-certified bamboo and postconsumer recycled paper, which makes it easily recyclable as well. The mixture is bound together using a water-based polymer resin that contains no solvents or VOCs. These countertops meet the standards set by other countertop materials, such as granite or butcher block. Its ease of fabrication also makes it a viable choice for wall coverings or flooring. The countertops can be manufactured in a variety of colors. All materials are sourced regionally, so projects within 500 miles of Puyallup, Washington, should qualify for the Regional Materials credit.

## LEED Credits

**+ MR 2**
Construction Waste Management

**+ MR 4**
Recycled Content

**+ MR 5**
Regional Materials

**+ MR 6**
Rapidly Renewable Materials

**+ MR 7**
Certified Wood

**⊞ IEQ 4.1**
Low-Emitting Materials—Adhesives and Sealants

### Information
Klip BioTechnologies, LLC
7314 Canyon Road East
Puyallup, WA 98371
T 253 507 4622
joel@kliptech.com
www.kliptech.com

# ecoX

## LEED Credits

**+ MR 4**
Recycled Content

**+ MR 5**
Regional Materials

**⊞ IEQ 4.1**
Low-Emitting Materials—
Adhesives and Sealants

### Information
meld USA
3001–103 Spring Forest Road
Raleigh, NC 27616
T 919 790 1749
F 919 790 1750
info@meldusa.com
www.meldusa.com

### What is it?
An environmentally friendly concrete blend for finish surfaces

### Where can I use it?
Countertops, tiles, stair treads, wall panels, pavers, fireplaces, benches

### Why is it green?
Postconsumer glass bottles and preconsumer fiberglass make up approximately 76 percent of ecoX. These materials are blended in with the company's proprietary concrete mix to create a visually stunning and durable surface that is then sealed with a low-VOC penetrating sealer that meets the requirements for low-emitting materials. All materials are sourced from within 500 miles of the company's manufacturing facility in Raleigh, North Carolina.

# EnviroMODE

**What is it?**
Terrazzo made from recycled materials

**Where can I use it?**
Floors, countertops

**Why is it green?**
This terrazzo is made from recycled bathtubs, sinks, and toilets, which are converted into porcelain pieces that are mixed with a resin to make a beautiful surface that is durable and environmentally sensitive. The composition is 100 percent postconsumer recycled content. The company offers dozens of colors, including natural earthy tones. The base material is broken down into pieces large enough to identify the original source.

## LEED Credits

✦ **MR 4**
Recycled Content

**Information**
EnviroGLAS
7704 San Jacinto Place
Suite 200
Plano, TX 75024
T 972 608 3790
communications@
enviroglasproducts.com
www.enviroglasproducts.com

# EnviroPLANK

## LEED Credits

**+ MR 4**
Recycled Content

**Information**
EnviroGLAS
7704 San Jacinto Place
Suite 200
Plano, TX 75024
T  972 608 3790
communications@
enviroglasproducts.com
www.enviroglasproducts.com

**What is it?**
Tiles made from recycled material

**Where can I use it?**
Flooring, backsplashes, wall coverings

**Why is it green?**
EnviroGLAS makes EnviroPLANK tiles using 100 percent postconsumer recycled glass and porcelain terrazzo. By binding the materials together with color pigments and an epoxy resin, the company is able to offer dozens of colors not found in the source material. The tiles are very large, at 6 x 36 inches, making installation fast and easy using standard methods.

# FLOR Carpet Tiles

### What is it?
Modular carpet tiles

### Where can I use it?
Anywhere you would use standard wall-to-wall or area carpeting

### Why is it green?
In order to meet the Low-Emitting Materials credit, any carpet system you use must meet the Carpet and Rug Institute's stringent testing standards for VOC levels. Carpet systems must meet the institute's Green Label Plus requirements, and carpet cushions must meet their Green Label program requirements for off-gassing. All of the FLOR carpet tiles meet the Green Label Plus requirements and can be mixed and matched as desired. Also, depending on the series of tile—there are about 70 lines at any given time—the product may contain recycled content or natural renewable fibers, like coir in the case of FLOR. These carpet tiles install easily without any adhesives and come with bull's-eye stickers to help you line them up perfectly. They can be cut to fit a curved space and can be removed as easily as they are installed.

InterfaceFlor, which produces FLOR, offers a revolutionary return-and-recycle program in which the tiles can be sent back to InterfaceFlor for proper disposal. The company never wants a tile to end up in a landfill.

### Special Considerations
*There is no minimum amount of carpet necessary to achieve the Carpet Systems credit.*

## LEED Credits

✦ **MR 2**
Construction Waste
Management

✦ **MR 4**
Recycled Content

✦ **MR 6**
Rapidly Renewable Materials

⊞ **IEQ 4.3**
Low-Emitting Materials—
Flooring Systems

### Information
InterfaceFlor
1503 Orchard Hill Road
LaGrange, GA 30240
T 800 336 0225
www.interfaceflor.com

# Fossil Limestone

## LEED Credits

**+ MR 3**
Materials Reuse

### Information
Green River Stone
116 Donlon Road
Fly Creek, NY 13337
T 607 547 5920
doug@greenriverstone.com
www.greenriverstone.com

**What is it?**
Natural stone containing fossils

**Where can I use it?**
Murals, backsplashes, countertops

**Why is it green?**
Green River Stone has a private quarry in southwest Wyoming where it extracts calcium carbonate shale peppered with eons-old fossilized aquatic life. All of the fossils are extracted according to the specifications set forth by the American Association of Paleontological Suppliers Code of Ethics, a kind of FSC certification for fossils.

According to paleontologists, the uplifted Rocky Mountains created a basin, now called Fossil Lake, some 50 million years ago. There are so many fossilized fish remains of different species that scientists believe there were events that killed a large number of fish at a time, and their remains settled at the bottom of a lake, each species in a distinct layer.

This stone comes in standard panel sizes of 2 x 3 feet and 4 x 5 feet for making backsplashes or murals, and much larger slabs can be custom ordered for countertops or tabletops. The material is roughly as durable as marble and naturally porous. It must be sealed so that food or liquid deposits do not stain it.

# FreeStyle SelecTile

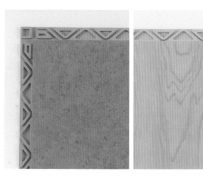  

### What is it?

Floating floor-tile system made from recycled content

### Where can I use it?

Flooring

### Why is it green?

FreeStyle Flooring's SelecTile floor tiles are made with 50 percent postconsumer recycled vinyl and carpet, making them easily recyclable. These tiles can be used to mimic a variety of looks, from bamboo to concrete to terracotta. The tiles are edged with an interlocking grid system and can lock together and be placed over an existing floor without the use of any adhesives. This makes the system as easy to use in new construction as in an existing building because you don't need to fix cracked floors or remove prior adhesives. The system comes up as easily as it goes down, so it can be reused over and over. The tiles are highly resilient and waterproof and will stay in place under a 250-psi load, making them perfect for high-traffic areas. To increase durability, a low-VOC flooring adhesive can be used to hold them in place.

### Special Considerations

*These will probably be best visually suited for a commercial space.*

## LEED Credits

✛ **MR 1.1**
Building Reuse—Maintain Existing Walls, Floors and Roof

✛ **MR 1.2**
Building Reuse—Maintain Existing Interior Nonstructural Elements

✛ **MR. 2**
Construction Waste Management

✛ **MR 4**
Recycled Content

### Information

FreeStyle Flooring
33 Wales Avenue
Unit F
Avon, MA 02322
T  508 583 3200
F  508 583 3260
contactus@selectechinc.com
www.selectechinc.com

# GlasStone

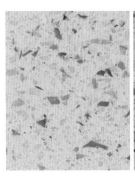  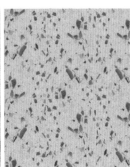 

## LEED Credits

+ **MR 4**
Recycled Content

+ **MR 5**
Regional Materials

⊞ **IEQ 8.1**
Daylight and Views—
Daylight

### Information
Clayton Block Companies, Inc.
111 Martins Lane
Trenton, NJ 08620
T  609 585 4422
www.claytonco.com

### What is it?
Concrete blocks containing recycled glass

### Where can I use it?
Exterior walls, interior walls

### Why is it green?
Among Clayton's many products is GlasStone, concrete masonry units (CMUs) containing recycled glass. The glass is a mixture of preconsumer and postconsumer recycled content, usually from window-factory leftovers and wine or beer bottles, respectively. The unique surface of these blocks is visually stunning; they don't need paint. They also reflect light, so if used creatively, they can help extend daylight further into a space, contributing to the Daylight and Views credit.

Clayton has locations all over the United States, but this product is manufactured at one of the New Jersey facilities. All materials are sourced locally, so if a project is anywhere in the Northeastern United States, GlasStone will likely qualify for the Regional Materials credit.

# Globus Cork Flooring

**What is it?**
Flooring made from the bark of the cork tree

**Where can I use it?**
Flooring

**Why is it green?**
Globus Cork manufactures cork flooring in two dozen colors, ranging from naturals to primaries, and uses only water-based binders and adhesives that contain no VOCs. Cork makes an excellent choice for flooring because of its resilience and beauty. It naturally produces a waxy substance called suberin, which makes the cork impervious to insects, gives it fire resistance, and prevents the cork from rotting even when it is completely submerged in liquid. This cork flooring can be applied in wet environments, such as bathrooms or kitchens, without concern for the durability of the flooring.

## LEED Credits

+ **MR 6**
Rapidly Renewable Materials

⊞ **IEQ 4.1**
Low-Emitting Materials—
Adhesives and Sealants

**Information**
Globus Cork
741 East 136th Street
Bronx, NY 10454
T 718 742 7264
F 718 742 7265
info@corkfloor.com
www.corkfloor.com

# Interstyle Recycled Glass Tile

## LEED Credits

**+ MR 2**
Construction Waste
Management

**+ MR 4**
Recycled Content

**Information**
Interstyle Ceramic & Glass
3625 Brighton Avenue
Burnaby, BC V5A 3H5
Canada
T  604 421 7229
F  604 421 7544
info@interstyle.ca
www.interstyle.ca

**What is it?**
Recycled-glass tiles

**Where can I use it?**
Walls, backsplashes

**Why is it green?**
Interstyle has three lines of recycled-glass tiles: the Aquarius, Agates, and River Crystals series, all made with 100 percent recycled glass. The tiles in the Aquarius series look like colored gems in suspension, while the Agates look like beautiful glass pebbles, and the River Crystals are like polished stones.

The company has been an environmental steward for a long time. It uses exhaust heat from its kilns to cure the tiles and uses recycled materials for packing its shipments. As the product is made from recycled glass, cutoffs or tiles broken during a project can be easily recycled.

# Jelly Bean Rocks

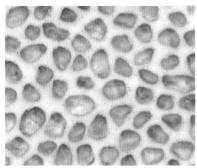

**What is it?**
Tiles made with recycled glass

**Where can I use it?**
Floors, walls, backsplashes

**Why is it green?**
These tiles are made with over 90 percent glass sourced from postconsumer recycled bottles. The bottles are crushed into small pieces and then tumbled smooth so they look like jelly beans. These are then mesh mounted on sheets. They come in 4 x 4 inch, 4 x 12 inch, and 12 x 12 inch pieces.

## LEED Credits

**+ MR 4**
Recycled Content

**Information**
Fireclay Tile Inc.
495 West Julian Street
San Jose, CA 95110
T 408 275 1182
F 408 275 1187
www.fireclaytile.com

# Kirei Coco

## LEED Credits

**✛ MR 4**
Recycled Content

**✛ MR 6**
Rapidly Renewable Materials

**✛ MR 7**
Certified Wood

### Information
Kirei USA
412 North Cedros Avenue
Solana Beach, CA 92075
T  619 236 9924
F  240 220 5946
info@kireiusa.com
www.kireiusa.com

**What is it?**
Tiles made from coconut shells

**Where can I use it?**
Wall coverings, flooring

**Why is it green?**
Coconuts are a rapidly renewable resource that is harvested annually. Most companies that harvest coconuts are only interested in the milk, the meat, and possibly the coir, the coarse fibers between the husk and the outer shell of the coconut, which are used for door mats, brushes, sacks, etc. Usually the shells are discarded or taken to a landfill. The shells are bound to a backing made from FSC-certified plywood using a low-VOC resin to make wall tiles. The tiles come in about a dozen different styles and can be mixed and matched to create different effects. They are available in 1 x 1 foot tiles and 4 x 4 foot panels.

**Special Considerations**
*These tiles are not flat and cannot be used as flooring.*

# Lonmetro UV

### What is it?
Vinyl flooring

### Where can I use it?
Flooring

### Why is it green?
Lonmetro UV is a vinyl-flooring material that is extremely durable and ideal for heavy-traffic commercial applications. It has a layer of UV-cured urethane, which gives it enhanced chemical resistance and makes it easy to maintain. The material is made of 35 percent preconsumer recycled content, so it counts as half in the credit calculations. It is available in several colors, and it is installed using standard methods. If a low- or no-VOC adhesive is used, the project will qualify for an additional credit in Low-Emitting Materials—Adhesives and Sealants.

### Special Considerations
*Vinyl flooring is a very durable choice and works well in commercial setting but may not be as appealing for residential use.*

## LEED Credits

+ **MR 4**
Recycled Content

### Information
Lonseal, Inc.
928 East 238th Street
Carson, CA 90745
T  310 830 7111
F  310 830 9986
info@lonseal.com
www.lonseal.com

# Luminescent Tile Strips

 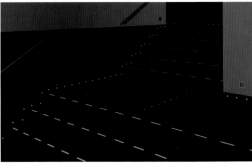

## LEED Credits

⊙ **SS 8**
Light Pollution Reduction

✳ **EA P2**
Minimum Energy Performance

✳ **EA 1**
Optimize Energy Performance

**Information**
Deutsche Steinzeug
America, Inc.
367 Curie Drive
Alpharetta, GA 30005
T 770 442 5500
F 770 442 5502
info@dsa-ceramics.com
www.dsa-ceramics.com

**What is it?**
Ceramic tiles with built-in luminescent strips

**Where can I use it?**
Flooring, walls

**Why is it green?**
These tiles incorporate a luminescent strip that cannot be damaged by dirt or high traffic. The tile strips will never run out of light, as they use the light that they absorb—natural or artificial—to provide illumination when it is dark. These tiles can be particularly helpful providing direction to emergency exits when power is lost or when smoke blocks out ceiling lights. Since these tiles can be used to illuminate steps, doorways, and other important areas without the use of electrical power, they will help comply with Light Pollution Reduction requirements, which stipulate that all nonemergency lighting typically be turned off during non-business hours.

# Milk Paint

**What is it?**
Paint made from all natural ingredients

**Where can I use it?**
Walls, ceilings, furniture, children's toys

**Why is it green?**
Using milk protein, lime, and clay as the base, then adding colored earth pigments like ochre, iron oxide, and lampblack, the Old Fashioned Milk Paint Company produces nontoxic paint in over twenty different colors. The paint is so safe that it probably wouldn't harm you even if you licked the walls.

The paint comes in powder form, to be mixed to the desired coverage level, from a light stain to a full cover coat. The paint contains zero VOCs, lead, mercury, petroleum by-products, plastics, or synthetic preservatives, and it is odorless once dry.

**Special Considerations**
*This paint may require several coats to achieve complete coverage.*

## LEED Credits

⊞ **IEQ 4.2**
Low-Emitting Materials—
Paints and Coatings

**Information**
The Old Fashioned Milk Paint
Co., Inc.
436 Main Street
Groton, MA 01450
T  978 448 6336
F  978 448 2754
sales@milkpaint.com
www.milkpaint.com

# Natural Cork Flooring

## LEED Credits

**+ MR 6**

Rapidly Renewable Materials

**Information**

Natural Cork, Inc.

T 800 404 2675

www.naturalcork.com

**What is it?**

Flooring made from cork

**Where can I use it?**

Flooring

**Why is it green?**

Cork is an excellent choice for flooring, not only because it is made from a renewable resource, but also because it gives any room a unique look. Cork is harvested every 9 years, but the tree is never destroyed—the farmer removes the bark without harming it. A tree that is over 100 years old can still produce beautiful and abundant cork. Cork has a nice resilience that you can feel when you walk on it, making it a great option for a work area or kitchen where someone might be standing in place for a long time. According to Natural Cork, its flooring uses a high density of cork, which gives it better resilience and sound-dampening properties. It installs like any floating flooring system and comes in a variety of colors and thicknesses.

# Nature's Carpet

**What is it?**

Carpet made from rapidly renewable material

**Where can I use it?**

Interiors

**Why is it green?**

Made from 100 percent New Zealand wool and completely biodegradable, this carpet easily qualifies for the Carpet and Rug Institute's Green Label Plus program, which sets standards for toxic off-gassing in carpets. Wool is not only rapidly renewable but also acts as an excellent natural insulator; its hygroscopic properties allow absorption and release of water as necessary to regulate the temperature. The backings for these carpets are made of jute, a rapidly renewable plant that is a natural alternative to synthetic rubber.

**Special Considerations**

*If the carpet is Green Label Plus certified it counts no matter how much you use.*

## LEED Credits

✛ **MR 2**
Construction Waste Management

✛ **MR 6**
Rapidly Renewable Materials

⊞ **IEQ 4.3**
Low-Emitting Materials—Flooring Systems

**Information**

Nature's Carpet
494 Railway Street
Vancouver, BC V6A 1B1
Canada
T 604 734 2758
F 604 734 1512
cecilia@naturescarpet.com
www.naturescarpet.com

# PaperForms

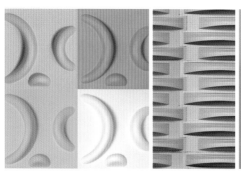  

## LEED Credits

+ **MR 4**
Recycled Content

**Information**
MIO
446 North 12th Street
Philadelphia, PA 19123
T  215 925 9359
info@mioculture.com
www.mioculture.com

**What is it?**
Recycled-paper wall covering

**Where can I use it?**
Interior walls, ceilings

**Why is it green?**
MIO has created PaperForms, a modular wall system that is made of 100 percent pre- and postconsumer waste paper. You can rotate the tiles, mix and match different colors, and paint them for the desired effect. The tiles are dimensional and add depth to an installation. They can be placed temporarily with double-sided tape or permanently with wallpaper adhesive. One pattern with several differently angled surfaces offers acoustic insulation properties by deflecting sound waves in various directions.

**Special Considerations**
*Since these are made of paper, they are not ideal for high-traffic areas, as any significant impact will crush the raised forms.*

# PaperStone

**What is it?**

Countertop surface made from recycled paper

**Where can I use it?**

Countertops, vanities, cladding, signs, partitions

**Why is it green?**

PaperStone is made of postconsumer waste paper mixed with a proprietary resin made from binders, like cashew nut shell liquid. The result is a countertop as hard as comparable surfaces like granite. There are two lines of PaperStone products: the Original series made from 100 percent postconsumer recycled cardboard and the Certified series made from 100 percent postconsumer office paper. The material comes from an FSC supply chain, so the trees that originally went into the office paper were harvested in a sustainably managed forest. All material is sourced locally, and the composites contain no added urea formaldehyde. The countertops are available in standard thicknesses of ¾ inch, 1 inch, and 1¼ inches.

## LEED Credits

✦ **MR 4**

Recycled Content

✦ **MR 5**

Regional Materials

✦ **MR 7**

Certified Wood

⊞ **IEQ 4.4**

Low-Emitting Materials—Composite Wood and Agrifiber Products

**Information**

PaperStone Products
2999 John Stevens Way
Hoquiam, WA 98550
T  360 538 9815
joan@paperstoneproducts.net
www.paperstoneproducts.com

# PapierTile

## LEED Credits

**+ MR 4**
Recycled Content

**⊞ IEQ 4.1**
Low-Emitting Materials—
Adhesives and Sealants

### Information
ARM Industries
45 Lewis Street
Binghamton, NY 13901
T  212 673 3027
F  646 225 5275

**What is it?**
An impermeable surface composite of recycled paper

**Where can I use it?**
Flooring, wall coverings, countertops

**Why is it green?**
PapierTile is a composite of recycled magazines, news-papers, and regular paper from office shredders bound with a proprietary environmentally friendly epoxy to create an impermeable surface with shredded paper suspended within it. The majority of this material is made up of postconsumer recycled content. The epoxy is VOC compliant, and thus there are no concerns about off-gassing. As an added bonus, the paper used in these tiles comes primarily from magazines with colorful glossy paper, which are notoriously difficult to recycle—some municipalities will not accept them at all. This material is available premade in 4 x 4 inch and 4 x 8 inch tiles or poured in place for a continuous floor or countertop.

# Recycled Tire Tiles

### What is it?
Floor tiles made from recycled tires

### Where can I use it?
Flooring

### Why is it green?
Recycled Tire Tiles are made from postconsumer recycled tires from large commercial vehicles. These tiles, $\frac{3}{8}$ inch thick, are very tough and can be used in high-traffic areas in commercial spaces or a home workspace. They are extremely comfortable to walk on and can be used to create a walk-off area outside entrances, where people can slough off dirt from their shoes before entering. As long as there's a regular maintenance schedule, this reduces the foreign pollutants that have a chance of making their way into your HVAC system.

## LEED Credits

✦ **MR 4**
Recycled Content

⊞ **IEQ 5**
Indoor Chemical and
Pollutant Source Control

### Information
Recycled Tire Tiles
T 614 372 8065
F 603 452 0301
sales@recycledtiretiles.com
http://recycledtiretiles.com

# Renewal

 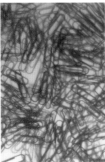  

## LEED Credits

**+ MR 3**
Materials Reuse

**+ MR 4**
Recycled Content

### Information
Fossil Faux Studios
1268 Folsom Street
San Francisco, CA 94103
T  415 621 6484
F  415 621 6082
www.fossilfaux.com

### What is it?
Surface material from recycled content

### Where can I use it?
Room dividers, wall coverings

### Why is it green?
Fossil Faux Studios makes architectural coverings and surfaces, a process that necessarily produces waste.
To mitigate the volume of leftover pieces and general office waste, the company decided to convert these items into beautiful, unique surfaces by encasing them in a custom resin. The surfaces contain up to 80 percent pre- or postconsumer content or reused materials. The scraps of waste material undergo minimal, if any, processing, so the original form of the recycled content is visible. One version contains used tea bags, another has scrap pieces of acrylic, and another has partially popped bubble wrap.

### Special Considerations
*Material appearance will vary.*

# Scintilla

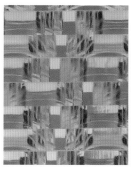

**What is it?**
Reflective wall paneling

**Where can I use it?**
Daylighting applications, wall coverings, furniture covering

**Why is it green?**
Scintilla is made completely from acrylic and is 40 percent preconsumer PETG (polyethylene terephthalate) by weight. Hundreds of light channels are carved into the acrylic, which creates an effect described by its manufacturer as a reconfiguring and diffusing of "moving shadows, producing unexpected rippling patterns." Using the principles of total internal light reflection—when light that hits a surface does not exit the other side but bounces around the inside of the reflector—the material redirects the light hitting it and refracts it in several directions.

A transparent exterior surface is the most straightforward way to get sunlight into a space. In places where there is a large floor plate and the sun's rays cannot reach deep into it, reflective surfaces can be used to redirect the light inward. This is exactly what Scintilla panels do. Furthermore, they not only enhance the incoming natural light, but also transform surfaces so that the walls that normally confine people become interactive.

The panels come in seven colors and are available in 4 x 4 inch, 4 x 8 inch, and 8 x 8 inch sizes at ½ inch thick, and 6 x 6 inch, 6 x 12 inch, and 12 x 12 inch at 1 inch thick.

**Special Considerations**
*Request a sample to see how the light will interact with this material where you intend to use it.*

## LEED Credits

**✦ MR 4**
Recycled Content

**⊞ IEQ 8.1**
Daylight and Views—
Daylight

**Information**
Sensitile Systems
1735 Holmes Road
Ypsilanti, MI 48198
T 313 872 6314
F 313 872 6315
info@sensitile.com
www.sensitile.com

# Scuffmaster

## LEED Credits

⊞ **IEQ 4.2**
Low-Emitting Materials—
Paints and Coatings

---

**Information**
Scuffmaster Architectural
Finishes
2777 Eagandale Boulevard
Eagan, MN 55121
T 800 898 0219
www.scuffmaster.com

**What is it?**
Low-VOC acrylic paint

**Where can I use it?**
Walls, ceilings

**Why is it green?**
Scuffmaster paints contain less then 150 g/L of VOCs, making them compliant with the Low-Emitting Materials credit. They offer several metallic and pearlescent colors that give texture to otherwise flat surfaces. They can also give a fresh, modern look to older materials—helpful in any green building project. The paint contains Microban antimicrobial protection, a nanotech coating that helps to protect surfaces from bacterial growth that might cause staining and health problems. The paint is also extremely durable: it has been tested to withstand 2,000 scrubs before wearing off.

# SpectraLOCK

**What is it?**

Tile grout

**Where can I use it?**

Floor tiles, wall tiles

**Why is it green?**

SpectraLOCK is just like standard tile grout—it spreads the same and has a working time (the period during which it is pliable) of 80 minutes. The difference is that SpectraLOCK has a very small amount of VOCs in it and is GREENGUARD certified. There is nothing toxic here.

## LEED Credits

⊞ **IEQ 4.1**

Low-Emitting Materials—
Adhesives and Sealants

**Information**

LATICRETE International, Inc.
One LATICRETE Park North
91 Amity Road
Bethany, CT 06524
T  203 393 0010
F  203 393 1684
info@sensitile.com
www.laticrete.com

# Starlight Photoluminescent Mosaic

## LEED Credits

⊙ **SS 8**
Light Pollution Reduction

✳ **EA P2**
Minimum Energy Performance

✳ **EA 1**
Optimize Energy Performance

### Information
Hispano Italiana de
Revestimentos, S.A.
Bº Borrancho, s/n
39110
Soto de la Marina
Cantabria
Spain
T +34 942 578006
F +34 942 578582
comercial@hisbalit.es
www.hisbalit.es

**What is it?**
Glow-in-the-dark tiles

**Where can I use it?**
Floors, walls, exit marking, wayfinding

**Why is it green?**
Hisbalit produces glow-in-the-dark, photoluminescent tiles. They can make identifying markings for rooms or emergency path indicators. Using these tiles means you might need to use less lighting, and therefore less energy. Absorbing natural or artificial light to provide self luminescence essentially doubles the amount of light from the same energy input.

One of the requirements for the Light Pollution Reduction credit is that nonemergency lights automatically shut off during nonbusiness hours. This product offers an option to reduce those lighting needs even further since it provides an alternative light source that allows the artificial lights to be turned off.

# TorZo Surfaces

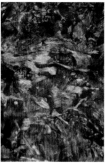 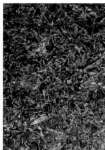  

### What is it?
Durable surface material

### Where can I use it?
Countertops, vanities, flooring, walls coverings

### Why is it green?
Torzo Surfaces makes architectural surfaces from several renewable and highly sustainable sources. It produces four lines that can be used for durable countertops and wall coverings. All the lines come in four different colors, Onyx, Cocoa, Copper, and Natural. The Indure series is made of a mix of 65 percent recycled wood chips and 35 percent acrylic resin. It has no added urea formaldehyde and qualifies for the Regional Materials credit, as all materials are sourced near the company's facility in Western Oregon. The Orient series is made from 75 percent recycled wood chips, and the remainder is acrylic resin. The Durum series is made from 70 percent rapidly renewable wheat stalks, which had been discarded and reclaimed, and using no added urea formaldehyde. The Seeta series is made from 70 percent sunflower seed hulls with no added urea formaldehyde. Sunflowers are a rapidly renewable resource, and their hulls are an agricultural waste product, making them an ideal material to recycle. Note that all of the recycled content used in these surfaces is preconsumer, so it counts for half in the LEED credit calculations.

## LEED Credits

+ **MR 4**
Recycled Content

+ **MR 5**
Regional Materials

+ **MR 6**
Rapidly Renewable Materials

+ **MR 7**
Certified Wood

⊞ **IEQ 4.4**
Low-Emitting Materials—
Composite Wood and
Agrifiber Products

### Information
Torzo Surfaces
2475 Progress Way
Woodburn, OR 97071
T 800 770 7523
F 503 971 7534
info@torzosurfaces.com
www.torzosurfaces.com

# Viridian Recycled Glass Tile

## LEED Credits

+ **MR 4**
Recycled Content

---

### Information
Modwalls
54 Old El Pueblo Road
Suite C
Scotts Valley, CA 95066
T  831 439 9734
F  831 439 9521
sales@modwalls.com
www.modwalls.com

### What is it?
Tile made from recycled glass

### Where can I use it?
Walls, floors, backsplashes

### Why is it green?
Glass that has been reclaimed and recycled from demolished buildings' windows, windshields, and window manufacturing makes up 98 percent of these tiles. The  tiles come in several colors and two finishes for use in various applications. The Industrial finish has a nonslip texture for high traffic areas; the Pearl finish has a slight sheen and is better suited for residential settings. Each tile is 1 square inch and comes mounted on sheets for easy installation, just like regular tiles.

# VOC Free Latex Paint

**What is it?**
Zero-VOC paint

**Where can I use it?**
Interior walls

**Why is it green?**
This is a latex paint with absolutely no VOCs. Although most people think that low-VOC paints are not as durable or do not cover as well as standard paints, the VOC Free Latex Paint spreads so well that you can apply it over an existing painted wall without a primer. It is also so durable that it can be used on kitchen and bathroom walls, and any dirt can be scrubbed off.

## LEED Credits

⊞ **IEQ 4.2**
Low-Emitting Materials—
Paints and Coatings

**Information**
Homestead House Paint
Company, Inc.
95 Niagara Street
Toronto, Ontario
M5V1C3
Canada
T 416 504 9984
F 416 504 9984
homesteadhouse@rogers.com
www.homesteadhouse.ca

# 6

# FURNISHINGS

# Environment Furniture

## LEED Credits

**+ MR 3**
Materials Reuse

**+ MR 4**
Recycled Content

**+ MR 7**
Certified Wood

### Information
Environment Furniture, Inc.
8126 Beverly Boulevard
Los Angeles, CA 90048
T  323 935 1330
F  323 935 1302
info@environment
furniture.com
www.environment
furniture.com

### What is it?
Furniture made from eco-sensitive natural materials

### Where can I use it?
Anywhere that furniture is needed

### Why is it green?
Environment Furniture makes various types of furniture, from beds to dining room tables to desks, from materials that are either reclaimed, recycled, or sourced from sustainably managed forests. The primary material in the furniture is peroba rosa, a hardwood from Brazil. The company sources this wood from abandoned structures, like monasteries in Paraná, Brazil, giving new life to materials with 70 to 100 years of history. It also uses a lot of Indonesian mahogany from a managed forest that is in the process of getting FSC certified. Finally, it employs recycled materials, such as particleboard that has been made from salvaged wood.

### Special Considerations
*Some of these pieces of furniture use dense wood and are very heavy, so installing and moving them may be a concern.*

# RD Legs

### What is it?
A chair made from recycled materials

### Where can I use it?
Wherever the need to sit arises

### Why is it green?
Using recycled postconsumer domestic plastic waste, such as beverage containers, Cohda handweaves the RD (Roughly Drawn) Legs chairs. No adhesives are used to hold these chairs together. At the end of their lives, they can easily be recycled. Each one of these chairs is unique.

### Special Considerations
*This product is not mass-produced and thus subject to availability.*

## LEED Credits

**+ MR 2**
Construction Waste Management

**+ MR 4**
Recycled Content

### Information
Cohda Design Limited
Studio 6, Design Works
William Street, Felling
Gateshead, Tyne and Wear
NE10 0JP
United Kingdom
T +44 1914 236247
F +44 1914 236201
info@cohda.com
www.cohda.com

# Reestore

## LEED Credits

**+ MR 3**
Materials Reuse

### Information
Reestore Ltd
2 Tamworth Building
Tythe Farm, School Lane
Colmworth, Bedfordshire
MK44 2JZ
United Kingdom
info@reestore.com
www.reestore.com

**What is it?**
Furniture made from everyday waste items

**Where can I use it?**
Anywhere that furniture is needed

**Why is it green?**
The design company Reestore has come up with clever ways to use things that have been discarded. The old adage that "one man's trash is another man's treasure" really holds true here, as this company makes couches out of bathtubs, chairs out of grocery carts, and a coffee table out of a washing machine drum. Their mission is to show that going green doesn't mean you have to compromise aesthetics or even use traditionally green materials. In this case, all you need is some trash.

**Special Considerations**
*The pieces are made in England and will have to be shipped to other countries.*

# Reinbarnation

**What is it?**
Furniture made from reclaimed barn wood

**Where can I use it?**
Anywhere that furniture is needed

**Why is it green?**
Roger Dinger is a salvager. He finds old derelict barns around North Carolina that are slated to be demolished and gets access to them so he can remove the wood and nails. He takes the materials and turns them into pieces of furniture—tables, benches, dressers, and almost anything else, since every item is custom made. Therefore no two pieces are alike, and each one contains a historical character only found in reused materials.

**Special Considerations**
*The manufacturer is an artist and will need time to create pieces for your project.*

## LEED Credits

**✛ MR 3**
Materials Reuse

**Information**
Roger Dinger
Siler City, NC 27344
T  919 542 4937
reinbarnation@msn.com
www.reinbarnation.com

# 7

# SPECIAL CONSTRUCTION

# AFS125

 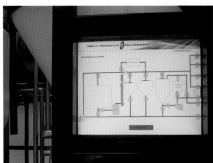 

## LEED Credits

⊙ **SS 4.3**
Alternative Transportation—
Low-Emitting and
Fuel-Efficient Vehicles

### Information
Allard Research and
Development, LLC
16276 County Road 616
Farmersville, TX 75442
T  972 782 6444
info@allardresearch.com
www.allardresearch.com

### What is it?
Alternative fuel production system

### Where can I use it?
Commercial parking areas, residential garages

### Why is it green?
One of the ways to achieve a LEED credit for low-emitting and fuel-efficient vehicles other than providing the vehicles or designating parking spaces for them is to provide the alternative fuel necessary to run those vehicles. Access to this type of site fueling, hopefully, will encourage people to use alternative vehicles. Many car manufacturers are producing vehicles that can run on some kind of *flex fuel*, a "flexible" ratio of petroleum gasoline and ethanol—usually made from corn, though other methods are being explored. Also, any car with a diesel engine can run on biodiesel—an alternative to petrol—which can be made from used cooking oil. (Incidentally, one of the first diesel engines ran on pure peanut oil.)

The AFS125 from Allard Research is the only fully automated miniature fuel refinery that can produce ethanol and biodiesel. With a footprint of just 24 square feet, the system can be installed anywhere, and the computer-controlled system will produce either type of fuel, or both at the same time, from used cooking oil and alcohol. It can make up to 120 gallons of ethanol or up to 450 gallons of biodiesel per day.

### Special Considerations
*Producing alternative fuel is great, if there are vehicles that can use it.*

# ASI THRU

**What is it?**
Semitransparent solar panel

**Where can I use it?**
Glass walls

**Why is it green?**
Photovoltaic cells provide energy from the sun, but there are often limitations involved in installing them. A roof may not be oriented in the proper direction, or, more commonly in urban areas, vandalism can be a major concern. SCHOTT takes the solar panels vertical by laminating them between two panels of glass. The entire glass facade of a building can become a solar energy generator. Because they are semi-transparent, the view to the outdoors is available to more spaces in the structure. They also block some of the thermal energy that would normally enter the space as heat, acting as an effective solar shade. ASI THRU provides all of the benefits of solar cells and glass walls in a more secure and reliable package than roof-mounted flat solar panels.

## LEED Credits

✳ **EA P2**
Minimum Energy Performance

✳ **EA 1**
Optimize Energy Performance

✳ **EA 2**
On-site Renewable Energy

⊞ **IEQ 8.1**
Daylight and Views—
Daylight

⊞ **IEQ 8.2**
Daylight and Views—
Views

**Information**
SCHOTT Solar AG
Tanja Brunner
Carl-Zeiss-Str. 4
63755 Alzenau
Germany
T +49 6023 91 05
F +49 6023 91 1700
solar.sales@schott.com
www.schottsolar.com

# BioStep

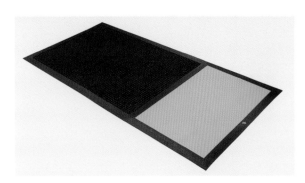

## LEED Credits

⊞ **IEQ 5**
Indoor Chemical and
Pollutant Source Control

### Information
Bio Environmental
Technologies, LLC
511 Broadway
Saratoga Springs, NY 12866
T 518 583 8999
F 518 514 1204
info@bioenvironmental
technologies.com
www.bioenvironmental
technologies.com

**What is it?**
Disinfecting entry mat

**Where can I use it?**
Outside entryways

**Why is it green?**
This mat is a delivery system for the manufacturer's disinfectant, BioCleen. In order to get the Indoor Chemical and Pollutant Source Control credit, a high level of air filtration is required, as is an entry system for removing pollutants from people's feet as they enter a home or commercial building. BioCleen is effective at neutralizing 99.1 percent of microorganisms before they have a chance to get inside the building. Keep in mind that when using an entry mat instead of a permanent grating system, a regular maintenance schedule is necessary to ensure continued pollutant control.

**Special Considerations**
*The BioCleen compound needs to be replenished on a regular basis.*

# Ecoblue Cube

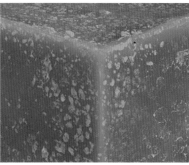

### What is it?
A cube that transforms urinals into waterless units

### Where can I use it?
Existing urinals

### Why is it green?
Ecoblue is a water-saving, porous material composed of billions of beneficial bacteria that break down natural waste into an odorless and easily manageable substance. Waterless urinals usually require some kind of cartridge to let liquid waste pass through without the use of any potable water. If you have a project with standard flushing units (typically using 1 to 1.6 gallons per flush) and want to convert it to a nearly waterless version, you no longer need to tear the units out, close off incoming water lines, and replace them with waterless fixtures. Now you can simply shut off the incoming water to the existing urinals and place one of these Ecoblue Cubes on top of the trap, and no more water gets wasted. At the end of each day, a maintenance person can turn the water on for one flush—that's it.

### Special Considerations
*Maintenance personnel will need to replace the cube approximately every six months, according to the manufacturer's specifications.*

## LEED Credits

💧 **WE P1**
Water Use Reduction

💧 **WE 3**
Water Use Reduction

### Information
Ecoblue
188 East Broadway Boulevard
Tucson, AZ 85701
T  877 326 2823
F  520 908 6593
info@ecobluecube.com
www.ecobluecube.com

# EnvIRONtread II

## LEED Credits

**+ MR 4**
Recycled Content

### Information
Arden Architectural Specialties
9300 73rd Avenue North
Brooklyn Park, MN 55428
T 763 488 9293
F 763 488 9294
sales@ardenarch.com
www.ardenarch.com

### What is it?
Open tread grate

### Where can I use it?
Entryways

### Why is it green?
For a project to qualify for the Indoor Chemical and Pollutant Source Control credit, there must be a permanent walk-off system installed for at least 6 feet in the direction of travel outside each entrance to a building. Someone walking in with dirty shoes would shuffle against these grates before entering a space, sloughing off all the grime and pollutants that would clog the HVAC system and, more importantly, people's lungs. Just for good measure, the rubber inserts in these grates are made from 59 percent postconsumer and 22 percent preconsumer recycled rubber that has been sourced from truck and airplane tires.

### Special Considerations
*These grates are considerably more expensive then simple welded grates but are cleaner, more attractive in appearance.*

# EZ Glide 350

**What is it?**
Synthetic ice-skating surface

**Where can I use it?**
Indoors, outdoors

**Why is it green?**
Ice skating rinks use an abundance of power: they require a lot of refrigerant, and making ice generates a great amount of waste heat. Ice skating rinks have never been green, until now. EZ Glide 350 is a synthetic skating surface that can be used for temporary or permanent installations and requires no power to install or maintain—it is put down and periodically waxed by hand. It is made from an exclusive polymer blend and has the look and feel of natural ice, proven acceptable by hockey players and figure skaters alike. The only maintenance required is keeping it clean and applying the EZ Glide Enhancer, a water-based lubricant, as needed.

The surface is shipped on pallets as panels, and the most popular model has dovetail edges so anyone can put them in place and hammer them together without any special tools or skills. The dovetail panels are 45 x 90 inches and are available in thicknesses of $\frac{1}{2}$ inch, $\frac{3}{4}$ inch, and 1 inch, depending on the application. The panels are made of a solid compound, so even if they get scratched up after years of use, they can be flipped over to a brand new surface.

This system of panels can increase revenue for an ice skating complex because it works all year round and in any weather.

**Special Considerations**
*Die-hard ice skaters may have trouble accepting a synthetic surface.*

## LEED Credits

* **EA P2**
Minimum Energy Performance

* **EA 1**
Optimize Energy Performance

* **ID 1**
Innovation in Design

**Information**
Multiplex Systems, Inc.
501 Furman Road
Suite A
Greenville, SC 29609
T 864 232 2591
ezinfo@ezglide350.com
www.coldproducts.com

# Hendrick Screens and Grates

## LEED Credits

⊙ **SS P1**
Construction Activity
Pollution Prevention

✦ **MR 2**
Construction Waste
Management

✦ **MR 4**
Recycled Content

⊞ **IEQ 5**
Indoor Chemical and
Pollutant Source Control

### Information
Hendrick Screen Company
3074 Medley Rd
Owensboro, KY 42301
T  270 685 5138
F  270 685 1729
sales@hendrickscreenco.com
www.hendrickscreenco.com

### What is it?
Recycled-content screens and grates

### Where can I use it?
Furniture, tree protection, water intakes

### Why is it green?
Hendrick Screen Company manufactures screens and grates for almost any application. All of its products contain some amount of pre- and postconsumer recycled content aluminum and steel. This composition makes them easily recyclable.

They can be used for stormwater grates to aid in drainage. There is a tree grate that goes around the base of a tree's trunk, protecting it from site disturbance during and after construction. If utilized in entryway systems, they can contribute to indoor chemical and pollutant control by sloughing dirt off the bottoms of people's shoes, preventing those particulates from entering the building and eventually the air handling systems.

### Special Considerations
*This product can create areas for dirt, dust, or debris to build up and may require extra cleaning.*

# Lumeta Solar Tiles

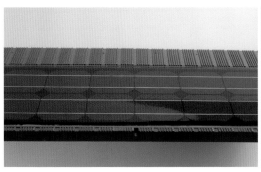

**What is it?**
Roof-tile-integrated solar panels

**Where can I use it?**
Roofing

**Why is it green?**
Solar panels are typically expensive to install and maintain, and can ruin even the most progressive of attractive roof lines with their boxy protruding appearance. Lumeta tries to solve that problem by integrating the solar cell into the roofing medium with its Solar Tiles. They currently come in two styles, a flat tile that looks like a standard clay tile (available in several colors) and the s-tile, a tile that when linked together looks like the letter *s* and has the appearance of terra-cotta. They offer an easy, attractive way to bring a source of on-site renewable energy to your project.

**Special Considerations**
*Solar cells only achieve LEED credit if they provide a minimum of 2.5 percent of the building's total energy use. This may require more cells than available roof area.*

## LEED Credits

✳ **EA P2**
Minimum Energy Performance

✳ **EA 1**
Optimize Energy Performance

✳ **EA 2**
On-site Renewable Energy

**Information**
DRI Companies
17182 Armstrong Avenue
Irvine, CA 92614
T 949 266 1990
F 949 266 1960
sales@dricompanies.com
www.dricompanies.com

# North Tiles

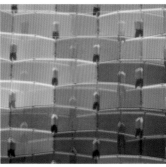

## LEED Credits

**✛ MR 6**
Rapidly Renewable Materials

**⊞ IEQ 6.1**
Controllability of Systems—
Lighting

### Information
Kvadrat A/S
Lundbergsvej 10
DK-8400 Ebeltoft
Denmark
T +45 8953 1866
kvadrat@kvadrat.dk
www.kvadrat.
headquarters.com

**What is it?**
Modular room-divider system

**Where can I use it?**
Office partitions, in place of permanent walls

**Why is it green?**
The tiles of this room-divider system are made from high-density foam covered in natural wool felt, a rapidly renewable resource. They come in over one hundred different colors, and they can be mixed and matched using a proprietary interlocking system of wings and flaps to create unique walls.

This wall system is so versatile and so easy to configure, disassemble, and reconfigure that an entire set of office partitions can be made out of these and still be adapted to each user's needs. Windows and doorways can be created in cubicles quickly by removing just a few of the tiles. As the sun moves throughout the day, the user could reconfigure the space during a 5-minute break and adjust the light or privacy as desired. It is also psychologically beneficial for a person to have control over the shape and structure of one's immediate environment.

**Special Considerations**
*These walls are meant to be used as dividers—they are not load bearing.*

# PowerPly

  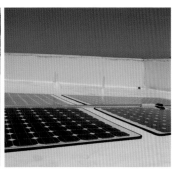

**What is it?**
Solar panels in sheet form

**Where can I use it?**
Roofing

**Why is it green?**
PowerPly is the closest thing to a peel-and-stick solar panel. These solar sheets have an adhesive back, making them 70 percent less expensive to install and requiring half the time it would take for standard solar panels. They also have no mounting hardware, and therefore avoid penetrating the roof, so there is less risk of leaks or thermal energy loss. They have a Teflon coating instead of glass, reducing their weight and providing better visual integration with a flat roof or pitched roof.

**Special Considerations**
*Solar panels need to provide a minimum of 2.5 percent of total power in order to qualify for LEED credit.*

## LEED Credits

✳ **EA P2**
Minimum Energy Performance

✳ **EA 1**
Optimize Energy Performance

✳ **EA 2**
On-site Renewable Energy

**Information**
DRI Companies
17182 Armstrong Avenue
Irvine, CA 92614
T 949 266 1990
F 949 266 1960
sales@dricompanies.com
www.dricompanies.com

# Smart Sponge

## LEED Credits

⊙ **SS 6.2**
Stormwater Design—
Quality Control

**Information**
Green Living Technologies, LLC
T 800 631 8001
F 585 467 1103
info@agreenroof.com
www.agreenroof.com

**What is it?**
Stormwater filtration system

**Where can I use it?**
Catch basins

**Why is it green?**
The Smart Sponge is a feat of engineering. Its molecular structure was developed to be chemically selective to hydrocarbons—so that it only bonds to hydrocarbons—and to destroy bacteria. This means it can remove oil from water and turn it into a nontoxic solid. The sponge does not require any mechanical systems and can be placed in any storm drain or catch basin. As contaminated water flows through the sponge, its structure permanently bonds with foreign contaminants, removing them from the flow. It stays buoyant even when fully saturated and works in fresh or salt water.

Aiding in waste management, the Smart Sponge can be used as an alternative fuel source for cement kilns. The natural debris, fuel and oil runoff, and dry matter that the sponge soaks up make it like a fire-starter log. Otherwise it must be sent to the landfill as solid waste.

**Special Considerations**
*The Smart Sponge's filter requires maintenance and must be replaced.*

# Solucent

**What is it?**
Architectural shading mesh

**Where can I use it?**
Exterior walls, interior partitions

**Why is it green?**
A shading mesh provides many of the same benefits as window shades: they prevent a substantial amount of the sun's thermal radiation from entering a building, thereby lowering cooling costs. The company states that this system can help realize energy savings of up to 23 percent. Solucent blocks the heat but still lets visible light through and allows people to see outside. This shading mesh adds a very attractive architectural element to projects. Solucent is also made using a high percentage of recycled materials as well as regional materials.

## LEED Credits

✴ **EA P2**
Minimum Energy Performance

✴ **EA 1**
Optimize Energy Performance

✛ **MR 4**
Recycled Content

✛ **MR 5**
Regional Materials

⊞ **IEQ 8.1**
Daylight and Views—
Daylight

⊞ **IEQ 8.2**
Daylight and Views—
Views

**Information**
Cambridge Architectural
105 Goodwill Road
Cambridge, MD 21613
T 866 806 2385
F 410 901 4979
sales@cambridge
architectural.com
www.cambridge
architectural.com

# Sphelar

## LEED Credits

* **EA P2**
Minimum Energy Performance

* **EA 1**
Optimize Energy Performance

* **EA 2**
On-site Renewable Energy

### Information

Kyosemi
949-2 Ebisu-cho
Fushimi-ku, Kyoto-shi 612-8201
Japan
T +81 75 605 7311
F +81 75 605 7312
www.kyosemi.co.jp

**What is it?**
Spherical solar cell

**Where can I use it?**
Producing energy on site

**Why is it green?**
These solar cells have a spherical shape, which makes them cheaper to produce and more efficient than traditional flat solar cells. To manufacture these cells the company takes molten silicone and lets it drip from a height of about 40 feet. A short burst of micro-gravity (an environment where only small gravitational forces are experienced) triggers crystallization and results in thousands of silicone spheres—this process actually makes them easier to produce than traditional flat panels. These spheres are then incorporated into a larger solar cell.

The sun changes positions throughout the day, so fixed solar panels can't always be oriented in the best direction, though this can be alleviated somewhat with a solar-tracking mechanism that shifts the panel automatically for optimal sun exposure. Any light that is reflected behind a flat panel or is diffused doesn't contribute power. The design of a spherical cell enables it to soak up energy from pretty much anywhere. Reflected or diffused light bounces off and around the spheres, dramatically increasing efficiency and generation of power—including when incorporated into window glass to create glass surfaces.

# TVM-5000

**What is it?**
Urban wind turbine

**Where can I use it?**
Urban rooftops

**Why is it green?**
In urban settings it is either impractical or in violation of building codes to put up typical propeller-style wind turbines. Many municipalities impose height restrictions that limit the effectiveness of these types of turbines, and birds can fly into them, creating mechanical issues for the turbines and more significant issues for the birds.

The Windation turbine has a footprint of 9 x 9 feet and stands only 11 feet tall. Each unit can provide enough electricity for 1,000 square feet of office space. The whole system is housed in a rectangular box, making it safe for birds. It runs quietly and can be installed quickly and easily due to its prepackaged design. Reduction of carbon footprint and increased use of renewable energy are essential in urban areas because that is where the majority of greenhouse gases are produced. The TVM-5000 provides a flexible solution for bringing renewable energy to cities.

## LEED Credits

\* **EA P2**
Minimum Energy Performance

\* **EA 1**
Optimize Energy Performance

\* **EA 2**
On-site Renewable Energy

**Information**
Windation Energy Systems, Inc.
contact@windation.com
www.windation.com

# Waterloo Biofilter

## LEED Credits

⊙ **SS 6.2**
Stormwater Design—
Quality Control

### Information

Waterloo Biofilter Systems Inc.
P.O. Box 400
143 Dennis Street
Rockwood, ON N0B 2K0
Canada
T  519 856 0757
F  519 856 0759
wbs@waterloo-biofilter.com
www.waterloo-biofilter.com

**What is it?**
Graywater and blackwater filter

**Where can I use it?**
Septic tanks, catch basins, treatment centers

**Why is it green?**
Polluted stormwater hits this filter medium and passes through it with the help of gravity. As the water passes through the filter, organic material is oxidized and ammonia is neutralized. This form of aerobic treatment renders pollutants harmless. The medium can also be used in septic tanks to treat seriously polluted wastewater. The medium is designed to process high loads of waste, typically ten times more than a comparable sand or soil filter. The Biofilter is capable of removing 85 to 98 percent of total suspended solids, 90 to 95 percent of biochemical oxygen demand, and 90 to 99 percent of coliform bacteria.

**Special Considerations**
*The filter medium must be replaced as needed.*

# Wovin Wall

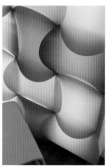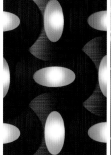

### What is it?
Modular tile system

### Where can I use it?
Walls, ceilings

### Why is it green?
Wovin Wall is a modular system that can be used to create wall and ceiling coverings with unique patterns easily and quickly without the use of special tools. The Pure Color series is made of 40 percent preconsumer recycled content, and the company offers tiles in wood veneer, polyresin, and aluminum finishes. The texture of these walls is highly distinct and visually stunning.

### Special Considerations
*Prices vary greatly depending on the finish chosen.*

## LEED Credits

✦ **MR 4**
Recycled Content

### Information
3form USA
2300 South 2300 West
Suite B
Salt Lake City, UT 84119
T 801 649 2500
F 801 649 2699
info@3-form.com
www.3-form.com

# 8

# MECHANICAL

# Cast Iron Pipe

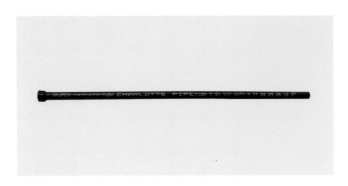

## LEED Credits

**+ MR 4**
Recycled Content

### Information

Charlotte Pipe and Foundry
Company
P.O. Box 35430
Charlotte, NC 28235
T 704 348 6450
F 800 553 1605
www.charlottepipe.com

**What is it?**
Recycled-content pipe

**Where can I use it?**
Rough plumbing

**Why is it green?**
Every year Charlotte Pipe diverts over 350 million pounds
of scrap iron and steel from the waste stream of the state of
North Carolina to use in its manufacturing process of cast-
iron pipes. The company also reuses 100 percent of its waste-
process water. Charlotte Pipe has a long-standing history as
a major supplier of cast iron pipes and fittings, which are
made from the recycled material that it keeps out of landfills.

**Special Considerations**
*The price of cast-iron pipes is subject to fluctuations that can
be affected by many variables, such as the weather and the
economy.*

# CeLPad

**What is it?**
Cellulose matrix for precooling air

**Where can I use it?**
Fresh-air intakes, windows

**Why is it green?**
CeLPad is a cellulose matrix that purifies, humidifies, and significantly cools the air that passes through it. It is ideally used to precool the air entering an air-conditioning system. For a space that is at 90 degrees to reach a more comfortable 72 degrees, normally the air-conditioning system would have to cool the air 18 degrees. If you install CeLPad, it will precool the air all the way down to that comfortable temperature, and then the air-conditioning system can simply circulate the air without expending any energy or adding a refrigerant to cool it. All that is required is to keep the CeLPad saturated with water. If the system is properly planned, you can completely eliminate the need for refrigerants or mechanical cooling. Furthermore, CeLPad is very portable, and if employees or residents place these in their windows, they can effectively control the temperature of their immediate environment.

**Special Considerations**
*Maintenance will be required to resaturate the CeLPad when it dries out.*

## LEED Credits

✳ **EA P2**
Minimum Energy Performance

✳ **EA P3**
Fundamental Refrigerant Management

✳ **EA 1**
Optimize Energy Performance

✳ **EA 4**
Enhanced Refrigerant Management

⊞ **IEQ 6.2**
Controllability of Systems—Thermal Comfort

⊞ **IEQ 7.1**
Thermal Comfort—Design

**Information**
HuTek (Asia) Co., Ltd.
91 Soi Akkaphat (Thonglor 17)
Vadhana, Bangkok 10110
Thailand
T +662 185 2831 4
F +662 712 6098
info@hutek-asia.com
www.hutek-asia.com

# Copper-Fin II

## LEED Credits

* **EA P2**
Minimum Energy Performance

* **EA 1**
Optimize Energy Performance

**Information**
Lochinvar Corporation World
Headquarters
300 Maddox Simpson Parkway
Lebanon, TN 37090
T  615 889 8900
www.lochinvar.com

**What is it?**
Efficient water heater

**Where can I use it?**
Water heating

**Why is it green?**
The Copper-Fin II is a highly efficient commercial water heater. One of the problems with water heaters is that they only operate at peak performance when they are running at maximum capacity. This heater is consistently 85 percent efficient at all capacities, which provides significant savings in energy costs. One of the ways the system is able to achieve this is through the system's copper-finned heat exchanger, the heater's namesake. The system uses a proportional firing system, meaning that it always provides the correct gas-to-air mixture (like a carburetor in a car) in response to the demand for hot water. All settings are computer controlled to ensure the best operation.

# CPC Evacuated Tube Solar Thermal Collectors

**What is it?**
Solar-powered hot-water heater

**Where can I use it?**
Roofs

**Why is it green?**
A couple of glass vacuum tubes, some copper piping, and a compound parabolic collector (CPC)—a curved mirror that focuses light—can produce one of the single most efficient ways to heat water. This system uses the thermal energy from the sun to preheat water before it enters a building's system to be used for radiant heating or domestic hot water. One or several of these arrays are placed on the roof of a building, or anywhere that they can get good sun exposure, and the incoming water from the building's main water source is slowly pumped through the array. The water moves through the tubes and collects solar energy—the simple act of the water moving through this fairly complex array is all it takes. The units require no electricity and have no moving parts.

In a conventional water-heating setup, 50-degree water (the typical temperature of ground water) enters a water heater and must be heated to around 120 degrees for domestic use. If the building has CPC Evacuated Tube Solar Thermal Collectors, the water could leave the solar heater at upward of 95 degrees. This would only require enough energy to produce a 25-degree temperature change instead of a 70-degree change, a roughly 65 percent reduction in energy usage.

**Special Considerations**
*Areas with minimal sun exposure will not be able to take advantage of this technology.*

## LEED Credits

💧 **WE P1**
Water Use Reduction

💧 **WE 3**
Water Use Reduction

✳ **EA P2**
Minimum Energy Performance

✳ **EA 1**
Optimize Energy Performance

**Information**
Schroder Zimmerly
P.O. Box 17532
Fort Mitchell, KY 41017
T  510 931 5786
F  267 295 8352
info@schroderzimmerly.com
www.schroderzimmerly.com

# DuctSox

## LEED Credits

✳ **EA P2**
Minimum Energy Performance

✳ **EA 1**
Optimize Energy Performance

⊞ **IEQ P1**
Minimum Indoor Air Quality
Performance

⊞ **IEQ 3.1**
Construction Indoor Air Quality
Management Plan—During
Construction

### Information
DuctSox Corporation
4343 Chavenelle Road
Dubuque, IA 52002
T 563 589 2777
mkluesner@ductsox.com
(Mary Jo Kluesner)
www.ductsox.com

### What is it?
Fabric HVAC ducts

### Where can I use it?
Open spaces, under floors, above ceilings

### Why is it green?
DuctSox are made from flexible, antimicrobial fabric and have many benefits over traditional metal ductwork. Whereas rigid metal ductwork has openings every few feet to provide adequate air flow, DuctSox have perforations along their entire length, so air is always distributed evenly over a greater area. This leads to more equally dispersed air and greater HVAC efficiency.

These flexible ducts can be shipped much more easily and hang from a rail system, making installation much simpler. In fact, a homeowner can completely remove them during the winter to recapture ceiling space if the system is only used for cooling. Since the fabric is porous to air, meaning the air is pushing out of the duct in all places, dust accumulation is prevented, and condensation, which can lead to mold growth, is not a factor. They also have a long usable life: unlike their rigid metal counterpart, because of their flexible nature, they will not be damaged if they are struck by objects, such as would be the case in a gymnasium.

### Special Considerations
*While they are not damaged by blunt force, DuctSox can be punctured by sharp objects.*

# EcoPower Faucets

**What is it?**
Self-powered automatic faucet

**Where can I use it?**
Bathrooms

**Why is it green?**
The Toto EcoPower faucet is the first automatic faucet that generates its own power for sustained operation. Most automatic-sensor faucets have batteries that need to be replaced over time, or they connect to building power supplies. The EcoPower uses the energy provided by the pressure of the water to turn a small turbine in its housing, which provides power and recharges its internal capacitors. Due to its self-contained design, it is easy to install and requires little to no maintenance.

Typical sensor faucets have an infrared sensor that is constantly on, and when they sense the presence of a person's hands, they activate and dispense a specified amount of water, even when the person's hands are no longer in front of the faucet. The EcoPower faucet uses a short infrared burst, rather than a constantly powered beam, which conserves energy. It also monitors its usage for the first week of operation to automatically determine times of low usage, when it can power down the sensor. Also, it stops the flow of water once a person pulls their hands away.

Federal guidelines require a low-flow faucet to dispense only 0.25 gallons per cycle. In a ten-second cycle the EcoPower faucet uses only 0.17 gallons, and since the faucet turns off when hands are pulled away, Toto estimates that typical usage is approximately 0.10 gallon per use.

## LEED Credits

◆ **WE P1**
Water Use Reduction

◆ **WE 3**
Water Use Reduction

✳ **EA P2**
Minimum Energy Performance

✳ **EA 1**
Optimize Energy Performance

**Information**
Toto USA, Inc.
1155 Southern Road
Morrow, GA 30260
T 770 282 8686
F 770 282 0002
humanres@totousa.com
www.totousa.com

# eco sac

## LEED Credits

♦ **WE P1**
Water Use Reduction

♦ **WE 1**
Water Efficient Landscaping

♦ **WE 2**
Innovative Wastewater
Technologies

♦ **WE 3**
Water Use Reduction

### Information
Waterplex Pty Ltd.
P.O. Box 59
Lane Cove NSW 1595
Australia
T +61 2 9113 5593
F +61 2 9113 5597
info@ecosac.com.au
www.ecosac.com.au

**What is it?**
Rainwater storage system

**Where can I use it?**
Gardens, basements, under decks

**Why is it green?**
A structure to capture rainwater can limit the need for municipal water by storing the rainwater to irrigate gardens, wash clothes, flush toilets, and possibly even produce potable water. The eco sac provides a storage system for the rainwater, and comes in sixty-six different sizes with capacities ranging from 450 to over 13,000 gallons. Unlike standard rain barrels, which take up a lot of room and can be unattractive, the eco sac is a flexible storage pod with a PVC liner that lies flat so it can fit in a crawl space or under an outdoor deck. They can also be daisy-chained together to increase capacity.

**Special Considerations**
*These storage containers need to be installed somewhere safe, where they don't run the risk of being punctured.*

# Equaris Water Recycling Center

 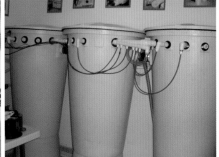 

**What is it?**
Small-scale water-treatment center

**Where can I use it?**
Graywater and wastewater treatment

**Why is it green?**
There are three parts to the Equaris water treatment system: the biomatter resequencing converter, graywater treatment system, and water-recycling center. If local codes allowed for it, these systems could eliminate the need for septic tanks or leach fields. The first two systems, which are completely automated and computer-controlled, can convert up to 95 percent of toilet waste and graywater to odorless carbon dioxide and water vapor. Using principles of aerobic and natural decomposition, the system neutralizes 99 percent of harmful pathogens, with a nearly 90 percent savings in water consumption. The remaining water vapor can then be sent to the water-recycling center, which utilizes another automated process of filtering and disinfection to produce potable water for household use or irrigation.

**Special Considerations**
*Calculate needs and usage as required for LEED submission.*

## LEED Credits

◆ **WE P1**
Water Use Reduction

◆ **WE 1**
Water Efficient Landscaping

◆ **WE 2**
Innovative Wastewater
Technologies

◆ **WE 3**
Water Use Reduction

**Information**
Equaris Corporation
15711 Upper 34th Street South
Afton, MN 55001
T 651 337 0261
F 651 337 0265
mail@equaris.com
www.equaris.com

# Nuheat Radiant

## LEED Credits

* **EA P2**
Minimum Energy Performance

* **EA 1**
Optimize Energy Performance

⊞ **IEQ 6.2**
Controllability of Systems—
Thermal Comfort

⊞ **IEQ 7.1**
Thermal Comfort—Design

### Information
Nuheat Industries
1689 Cliveden Avenue
Delta, BC V3M 6V5
Canada
T 800 778 9276
F 604 529 4404
central@nuheat.com
www.nuheat.com

**What is it?**
Radiant-heating system

**Where can I use it?**
Under flooring

**Why is it green?**
Heating a space from the floor up provides a more precise and even control over the temperature in a particular space than baseboard heaters or ceiling ducts. The Nuheat mats are placed on the floor and encased in a layer of mortar before the flooring is installed. These mats have no moving parts; an electrical current heats a single wire in the mats, which radiates the heat throughout the floor. The system uses Energy Star–rated thermostats, and users can selectively power small sections, heating only the rooms that are occupied rather then an entire structure, resulting in lowered energy demand. Because the system is modular, the heating can be limited to only the critical areas of a room. For example, it could be put in a bathroom under the tiles just outside the shower so the floor will be warm under bare feet as the user steps out of the shower. It can even be used outside to keep a stone patio warm for a cozy outdoor sitting area.

**Special Considerations**
*Once installed, this type of system cannot be altered without removing the entire floor.*

# Quench Shower System

**What is it?**
Water-saving shower

**Where can I use it?**
Showers

**Why is it green?**
A lot of people like taking long hot showers in the morning to wake up or at the end of a long day to relax, but many are trying to cut down on their water usage. Quench Solutions states that the Quench Shower System can save 82 percent on water use and up to 87 percent on energy usage. The Quench Shower allows you to take as long of a shower as you want, with minimal waste.

Users get in and operate the shower just as they would normally. The process of actually cleaning yourself in the functional part of the shower should only take about 2 minutes and use about five gallons of water. Once you are clean, you simply close the drain and let the reservoir—an indent in the floor of the shower around the drain—flood to the fill line with about a gallon of water. Then turn off the shower, and push a button on the shower body. The shower will recirculate filtered, temperature-controlled, and pressurized water from that reservoir for as long as you want, using no additional water and significantly less energy. When you're done, you release the drain and activate the sanitize-rinse cycle, which cleans the entire system.

**Special Considerations**
*Limited availability. Currently available in Australia only.*

## LEED Credits

💧 **WE P1**
Water Use Reduction

💧 **WE 3**
Water Use Reduction

✳ **EA P2**
Minimum Energy Performance

✳ **EA 1**
Optimize Energy Performance

**Information**
Quench Solutions Pty Ltd.
P.O. Box 41
Patterson Lakes, Victoria 3197
Australia
T +03 9786 7887
www.quenchshowers.com

# Rainwater HOG

## LEED Credits

◆ **WE P1**
Water Use Reduction

◆ **WE 1**
Water Efficient Landscaping

◆ **WE 2**
Innovative Wastewater
Technologies

◆ **WE 3**
Water Use Reduction

✚ **MR 2**
Construction Waste
Management

### Information
Rainwater HOG
402 Redwood Ave
Corte Madera, CA 94925
T 888 700 1096
info@rainwaterhog.com
www.rainwaterhog.com

### What is it?
Modular stormwater storage system

### Where can I use it?
Under decks, outside

### Why is it green?
We waste so much water, and sometimes reducing usage is more difficult than finding a better source. Stormwater that would have just run off into the ground—or worse, into the municipal sewer system—is perfect for irrigation, toilet flushing, and even laundry.

The Rainwater HOG is made from virgin polyethelene, which is a completely recyclable food-grade plastic. The inventor designed the system because he was frustrated with standard rain barrels, as they could only be placed in one orientation and did not fit under decks. Rainwater HOG tanks are designed to hold 51 gallons in a 9 x 20 inch footprint, enabling them to fit between joists under a deck or stand upright in a garden or against a building. Regardless of how they are placed, they can support their weight and will not bulge. They can also be strung together to offer unlimited capacity for stormwater capture. Once the tanks are in place, a standard garden hose can be attached for irrigation, or a supply line can be run back into the structure to fulfill domestic needs.

### Special Considerations
*Plan how much rainwater you will need to use when sizing this system.*

# Sink Positive

### What is it?
A sink that uses incoming clean water before it moves into the toilet tank

### Where can I use it?
Bathrooms

### Why is it green?
The Sink Positive is such a simple, obvious design. Every time you flush a standard toilet, water drains from the tank while fresh, clean water is brought back in the tank to fill it up, ready for the next flush. The Sink Positive installs on top of standard toilet tanks and redirects that incoming water flow through a small faucet, enabling you to wash your hands with clean water after flushing the toilet. That water, now considered graywater because of the soap in it, flows into the tank, ready for the next flush. The soapy water can have the added benefit of keeping your toilet bowl clean with each flush. If the toilet is located in a small bathroom where space constraints exist, you can eliminate a separate sink completely because the Sink Positive, placed on the toilet tank, will be enough.

The company estimates that by using the Sink Positive an individual can save one gallon of water each day. If everyone in the United States saved one gallon per day, that would equal approximately 900,000,000,000,000,000 gallons per year, or enough to fill Lake Superior thirty times.

## LEED Credits

◊ **WE P1**
Water Use Reduction

◊ **WE 3**
Water Use Reduction

### Information
Environmental Designworks
T 615 217 8066
support@sinkpositive.com
www.sinkpositive.com

# Soybean Based Urinal

## LEED Credits

💧 **WE P1**
Water Use Reduction

💧 **WE 1**
Water Efficient Landscaping

💧 **WE 2**
Innovative Wastewater
Technologies

💧 **WE 3**
Water Use Reduction

✦ **MR 6**
Rapidly Renewable Materials

### Information
Waterless Co.
1050 Joshua Way
Vista, CA 92081
T 760 727 7723
sales@waterless.com
www.waterless.com

**What is it?**
Waterless urinal made from soybean resin

**Where can I use it?**
Bathrooms

**Why is it green?**
Waterless urinals, as the name suggests, require no water in order to function—they only need to be hooked up to a drain. Most urinals use 1 gallon each time they are flushed, so replacing conventional urinals with waterless versions can save thousands or even tens of thousands of gallons each year. The Soybean Based Urinal uses Waterless Company's patented EcoTrap insert, which works by passing the urine through a liquid layer called BlueSeal, the company's proprietary agent BlueSeal forms a vapor barrier so that the odor from the liquid waste is contained.

There are other waterless urinals on the market, but this company takes things a step further and forms their urinals from 30 percent ENVIREZ, a soybean-based resin, a rapidly renewable material. Three ounces of BlueSeal last for 1,500 "passes," and the cartridge can be refilled without contact with the filter, which makes the units more sanitary. The cartridge needs to be replaced two to four times a year, and that is the extent of maintenance. Since there is no flush-o-meter and no moving parts, there isn't anything to repair.

**Special Considerations**
*Some local municipal codes may not allow waterless urinals.*

# SSG Thermovit Elegance

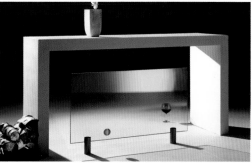

**What is it?**
Glass radiator

**Where can I use it?**
Room heating

**Why is it green?**
SSG Thermovit Elegance is a large sheet of specially made glass that serves as a room heater. There are two different models: a transparent one that disappears into a room, and a mirrored or patterned version that adds to the decor. To make the sheets, two 0.24 inch ( 6 mm) sheets of safety glass are laminated onto a 0.04 inch (1 mm) layer of polyvinyl butyral film. On one side of the glass, a conductive coating allows heat to be radiated in a specific direction rather than in all directions, which is less efficient. These radiators are 100 percent efficient because any "waste" electricity would be used as heat, and they come with a companion thermostat that accurately controls the heaters' output. They come in a variety of sizes.

**Special Considerations**
*There is a risk that someone may not notice the radiator and inadvertently break it.*

## LEED Credits

✳ **EA P2**
Minimum Energy Performance

✳ **EA 1**
Optimize Energy Performance

⊞ **IEQ 6.2**
Controllability of Systems—
Thermal Comfort

⊞ **IEQ 7.1**
Thermal Comfort—Design

**Information**
Compagnie de Saint-Gobain
Les Miroirs
18, Avenue d'Alsace
92400 Courbevoie
France
T +33 1 47 62 30 00
www.saint-gobain.com

# Steril-Zone Air Purifier

## LEED Credits

⊞ **IEQ P1**
Minimum Indoor Air Quality
Performance

✳ **ID 1**
Innovation in Design

**Information**
Steril-Aire, Inc.
2840 North Lima Street
Burbank, CA 91504
T 818 565 1128
sales@steril-zone.com
www.steril-zone.com

**What is it?**
Ultraviolet air purifier

**Where can I use it?**
Any room

**Why is it green?**
The Steril-Zone Air Purifier implements a three-stage process to eliminate airborne pollutants. It uses ultraviolet light to kill bacteria, viruses, and mold—physically filtering out pollutants rather than neutralizing them, something conventional filters can't do. It also uses an activated carbon filter to rid the space of bad odors and VOCs. The unit dramatically increases the indoor air quality of a space with almost immediately noticeable effects. Residents of buildings with air filtration have reported lower incidences of allergies and even asthma.

The LEED-certified City Hall in Sammamish, Washington, was the first to successfully use an ultraviolet air-filter technology—the Steril-Zone Air Purifier—to achieve an Innovation in Design credit, setting the precedent for other projects to incorporate this technology.

**Special Considerations**
*This additional equipment may require maintenance.*

# Synergy3D

**What is it?**
Efficient heat and hot water system

**Where can I use it?**
Commercial, residential settings

**Why is it green?**
The Synergy3D is a geothermal HVAC, hot water, and radiant heating in one system. The earth generally hold its temperature very well; the relationship between the earth's temperature and the temperature inside a space can be manipulated to regulate the indoor environment. Synergy3D employs a loop with a special fluid in it that has the ability to absorb or release heat in the ground—simply stated, when cooling is needed, the system can remove heat from a building and release it into the ground and vice versa when heating is needed. These types of systems can be between 300 to 400 percent more efficient because the pump that moves the fluid through the loop requires very little energy. Synergy3D uses this heat pump technology to provide heating and air conditioning, as well as domestic hot water, which can be used for radiant heating. The system combines the best aspects of forced hot air and radiant heating to create one of the most efficient systems possible.

The units come in sizes from 3-to-6 tons and use the very environmentally friendly R-410A refrigerant, qualifying it for Fundamental Refrigerant Management and possible Enhanced Refrigerant Management credits. If sufficient thermostats to provide individual control and an air filtering system, such as the ultraviolet verison offered by Steril-Aire, are added, the system can achieve two more credits in controllability and innovation.

## LEED Credits

**✳ EA P2**
Minimum Energy Performance

**✳ EA P3**
Fundamental Refrigerant Management

**✳ EA 1**
Optimize Energy Performance

**✳ EA 4**
Enhanced Refrigerant Management

**⊞ IEQ 6.2**
Controllability of Systems—Thermal

**⊞ IEQ 7.1**
Thermal Comfort—Design

**✳ ID 1**
Innovation in Design

**Information**
WaterFurnace International, Inc.
9000 Conservation Way
Fort Wayne, IN 46809
T 800 934 5160
F 260 474 5780
www.waterfurnace.com

# 9
# ELECTRICAL

# Eleek Lighting

## LEED Credits

⊙ **SS 8**
Light Pollution Reduction

+ **MR 4**
Recycled Content

+ **MR 5**
Regional Materials

### Information
Eleek Inc.
2326 North Flint Avenue
Portland, OR 97227
T  503 232 5526
F  503 232 5527
info@eleekinc.com
www.eleekinc.com

**What is it?**
Recycled-content light fixtures

**Where can I use it?**
Interior lighting, exterior lighting

**Why is it green?**
Eighty percent of the materials Eleek uses come from within 50 miles of its factory in Portland, Oregon. This means that projects built pretty much anywhere in the Northwest of North America can apply the use of Eleek Lighting—as an application of regional materials—toward LEED credit. Most of Eleek Lighting's fixtures are made from a mix of recycled bronze and recycled aluminum, though the specifics vary by fixture.

Some of the Eleek designs do not allow light to project horizontally onto other properties, which reduces light pollution. In interiors, the beam of light from a fixture should not hit a transparent surface like a window, which lets light pass to neighboring properties. This can be solved by using cut-off fixtures, which direct all the light downward. Additionally, the employment of cut-off shades made of dark materials, which are non-reflective, will keep the sky dark and the stars bright.

**Special Considerations**
*When designing lighting with minimal light pollution, keep in mind that the building occupants are the primary concern and that adequate working light is key.*

# Hyperion

### What is it?
Small-scale nuclear-power generator

### Where can I use it?
To power an entire city

### Why is it green?
Hyperion is essentially a "backyard" nuclear power plant. This is not just a concept; it is expected to be on the market within the next 5 years. Nuclear power provides about 20 percent of the energy in the United States; in France that number is closer to 80 percent. It is a widely used, extremely long-lasting power source.

Each unit is about the size of a hot tub, so it can be easily transported by truck or rail to neighborhood developments or remote off-grid projects. Each unit is sealed upon delivery, incapable of having a meltdown because of the small amount of nuclear material, and able to produce 25 MWe (megawatt electrical), enough to power 20,000 average-size homes. The unit produces zero greenhouse gas emissions and will last about 5 years because its core is only a couple dozen pounds and it has such a small amount of fuel in it (a fact that makes it even safer)—a typical nuclear power core weighs thousands of pounds and can last millennia. At the end of its life, it can be refueled at the original factory. This is green power generation for the future.

### Special Considerations
*The idea of a nuclear reactor in your backyard may be fascinating to some and terrifying to others. Also, since this product is not yet available, you won't be able to start building it into a project just yet.*

## LEED Credits

* **EA P2**
Minimum Energy Performance

* **EA 1**
Optimize Energy Performance

* **EA 2**
On-site Renewable Energy

### Information
Hyperion Power Generation
369 Montezuma Avenue
Suite 508
Santa Fe, NM 87501
T 505 216 9130
info@hyperionpower
generation.com
www.hyperionpower
generation.com

# Ilumisys MK1

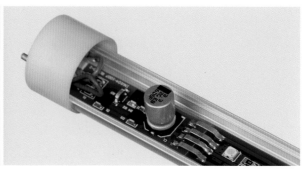

## LEED Credits

* **EA P2**
Minimum Energy Performance

* **EA 1**
Optimize Energy Performance

### Information
Altair Engineering, Inc.
1820 East Big Beaver
Troy, MI 48083
T  248 614 2400
F  248 614 2411
www.ilumisys.com

### What is it?
Efficient fluorescent-tube replacement

### Where can I use it?
In place of fluorescent tubes

### Why is it green?
The ilumisys MK1 looks like a fluorescent tube, but it is illuminated by light-emitting diodes (LEDs) instead of electrically charged mercury gas like standard fluorescent tubes are. These bulbs use no mercury and are a direct replacement for fixtures with standard T8 ballasts. Two of their models work without ballasts, making them an ideal replacement for T12 fixtures, the most standard type of fixtures in office and retail settings. LEDs are one of the most efficient lighting sources available to us today, and these bulbs put out the equivalent of 32-watt T8 fluorescent bulbs. While the company does not publish the exact wattage of the MK1, as an LED light source, you can safely assume it is at worst a third of its counterparts. These bulbs put out 1,400 lumens in different color temperatures (rather than just the very cool color temperature of fluorescent lights, which is the reason that they make skin look blue) and have a lifespan of 60,000 hours.

### Special Considerations
*The light that LED lighting gives off is unappealing to some and should be tested before you commit to it.*

# LEC Panels

**What is it?**
Flexible light panels

**Where can I use it?**
General lighting, task lighting, architectural lighting

**Why is it green?**
The underlying technology that powers LEC Panels is a closely held secret called Light Emitting Capacitors. These filmlike panels are just 0.04 inches (1 mm) thick and are completely flexible, or they can be made rigid with a backing. They are available in any dimensions up to 18 square feet (1.67 square meters) and provide bright, evenly distributed light using very little energy and without giving off heat. As a major lighting source the panels will lower energy demand, and as task lighting they can go places standard lamps cannot, such as under low shelves or inside small drawers.

**Special Considerations**
*These products are custom made and will be subject to some lead time.*

## LEED Credits

✴ **EA P2**
Minimum Energy Performance

✴ **EA 1**
Optimize Energy Performance

⊞ **IEQ 6.1**
Controllability of Systems—
Lighting

**Information**
CeeLite
66 Bethlehem
Pike Colmar, PA 18915
T 610 834 4190
F 610 285 8241
www.ceelite.com

# LightPoints

## LEED Credits

⊙ **SS 8**
Light Pollution Reduction

✳ **EA P2**
Minimum Energy Performance

✳ **EA 1**
Optimize Energy Performance

### Information
Schott North America, Inc.
555 Taxter Road
Elmsford, NY 10523
T  914 831 2200
F  914 831 2201
www.us.schott.com

### What is it?
LED glass

### Where can I use it?
Interior lighting, exterior lighting, accent lighting, glass

### Why is it green?
Schott is a company that has taken LEDs and encapsulated them in very strong laminated glass. The glass has an electrically conductive clear coating that wirelessly powers the diodes. The resulting product, LightPoints, creates an incredible effect: there are no wires, and the lights appear to be floating like stars in the sky. This material reduces the need to have external lights and uses very little energy itself. This also means there is very little that can go wrong since everything is encapsulated and there are very few parts. These systems can operate for decades without any problems.
The lights can be placed in locations you could not install traditional lighting fixtures, such as stair treads, elevator doors, walkways, and storefronts.

### Special Considerations
*This is a decorative product as much as a lighting product, and the primary focus should be on the design.*

# Solar LED Paver Lights

### What is it?
Solar-powered paver lights

### Where can I use it?
Path lighting, stair lighting

### Why is it green?
Solar LED Paver Lights soak up the sun's energy during the day in order to power LED lights at night. They require no electrical hookup and are completely self-contained, which makes installation simple and maintenance limited. LEDs are incredibly efficient: the company estimates that after a sunny day these pavers can provide light for 12 hours, and on a cloudy day that number drops to a still-respectable 5-to-8 hours. The lights automatically turn on when it is dark.

The LEDs provide adequate illumination for safety or decorative purposes, and because the light does not travel very far, they meet the requirements of light-pollution reduction. The pavers are housed in cast aluminum and come in 4 x 4 inch and 6 x 6 inch sizes, with white-, amber-, red-, blue-, or green-colored lights.

### Special Considerations
*These units are not an alternative to area lighting, just a supplement.*

## LEED Credits

⊙ **SS 8**
Light Pollution Reduction

✳ **EA P2**
Minimum Energy Performance

✳ **EA 1**
Optimize Energy Performance

### Information
ILOS Corporation
360 East 72nd Street
B300
New York, NY 10021
T  305 484 4972
F  305 471 7636
www.meteor-lighting.com

# INDEX

# LEED Credit Index

# Product Index

## Product Index (continued)

# Manufacturer Index

# Manufacturer Index (continued)